An Introduction to the
Psychology of Children's Drawings

An Introduction to the Psychology of Children's Drawings

GLYN V. THOMAS and ANGÈLE M. J. SILK

NEW YORK UNIVERSITY PRESS
Washington Square, New York

First published in the U.S.A. in 1990 by
NEW YORK UNIVERSITY PRESS
Washington Square
New York, NY 10003

Printed and bound in Great Britain by
Billing and Sons Limited, Worcester

Library of Congress Cataloging-in-Publication Data

Thomas, Glyn V., 1946–
    An introduction to the psychology of children's drawings/Glyn
V. Thomas and Angèle M. J. Silk
        p. cm.
    Includes bibliographical references.
    ISBN 0-8147-8184-5   ISBN 0-8147-8186-1 (pbk)
    1. Children's drawings — Psychological aspects.   2. Silk, Angèle
M. J., 1959–   I. Title
BF723.D7T48   1990   89–48701
155.4 — dc20   CIP

1   2   3   4   5   94   93   92   91   90

For Siôn and Dyfed

GVT

For Graham

AMJS

Contents

Preface

Our aim in this book has been to provide a selective review of psychological theories of children's drawings and some important recent research. The book is intended primarily for students of psychology who need an introduction to this aspect of child development, but also for teachers in schools and art colleges who need a concise, well-referenced and up-to-date source of information on psychological approaches to children's drawings.

There have recently been important developments in the psychology of children's drawings and we felt the lack of a single book which adequately surveyed the field. Recent books which have presented important new theoretical perspectives and new research findings have generally been too specialized or too technical for the readership and purposes we have in mind. Furthermore, many earlier works on children's drawings have often presented only one theoretical approach at the expense of alternatives.

We hope that the present book will provide a comprehensive introduction to this increasingly important area of study and provide sufficient references for interested readers to pursue their studies further.

A number of people have helped us in our work. We particularly wish to thank Ros Bradbury, George Butterworth, Norman Freeman, Tom Freeman and Elizabeth Robinson for their comments on earlier versions of the manuscript. They have all helped us to improve the book, but are in no way to blame for any shortcomings. We also wish to thank all the children who have helped us in the past with our researches and who have charmed us with the humour and sensitivity of their drawings.

Acknowledgements

We gratefully acknowledge the permission to use the following material:

Arnheim, R. (1956) *Art and Visual Perception: A Psychology of the Creative Eye*, London: Faber & Faber.

Arnheim, R. (1969) *Visual Thinking*, London: Faber & Faber.

Bremner, J. G. and Taylor, A. J. (1982) 'Children's errors in copying angles: perpendicular error or bisection error?', *Perception*, 11, 163–71.

Carothers, T. and Gardner, H. (1979) 'When children's drawings become art: the emergence of aesthetic production and perception', *Developmental Psychology*, 15, 570–80.

Gardner, H. (1980) *Artful Scribbles: The Significance of Children's Drawings*, New York: Basic Books.

Gibson, J. J. (1979) *The Ecological Approach to Visual Perception*, Boston: Houghton Mifflin.

Goodman, N. (1976) *Languages of Art* (2nd edn), Indianapolis: Hackett.

Hammer, E. F. (1958) *The Clinical Application of Projective Drawings*, Springfield, Ill.: C. C. Thomas.

Koppitz, E. (1968) *Psychological Evaluation of Children's Human Figure Drawings*, London: Grune & Stratton.

Piaget, J. and Inhelder, B. (1969) *The Psychology of the Child*, London: Routledge & Kegan Paul.

Wiltshire, S. (1987) *Drawings*, London: J. M. Dent.

Introduction

Have you ever looked at a child's drawing and wondered what it reflects of the young artist's thoughts and feelings? Children's drawings have an immediate appeal: they are simple and charming, full of life and character. On closer inspection, however, these drawings often have queer, even disturbing, features. Take a look at Figures 1 and 2. What does it mean, for example, if a person is drawn with the arms coming out of the side of the head, or if the body and arms are missed out altogether? In the past, psychologists' answers to such questions often appealed vaguely to children's immature concepts or emotional states. Thus, for example, arms drawn coming out of the side of the head were claimed to reflect an immature concept of the human figure. Because such interpretations really did not explain anything and did not lead to rigorously defined and testable propositions, research into children's drawing for many years made only limited progress. Recently, however, there have been two important changes which have revitalized the study of children's drawings: first, the once popular naturalistic approach of describing large numbers of drawings has mainly been replaced by experimental investigations in which children have been set carefully designed drawing tasks in an attempt to answer specific questions; and second, we have recently become aware of the importance of the drawing process in determining the final shape of the finished drawing.

The combined effect of these changes has been to open up new and exciting areas of enquiry and to breathe new life into many old ones. A major theme of this book is to convey something of the enormous progress that has been made recently as a result of these changes in approach. In the first two chapters we try to acquaint the reader with the main features of the subject area by presenting a brief history of research into children's drawing, an overview of the main theoretical approaches and a description of the principal characteristics of children's drawing at different ages. Each chapter then considers a particular question about children's drawing.

Chapter 3 deals with the surprisingly difficult question of what a drawing is. Our discussion begins with the ways artists, philosophers and perceptionists have conceptualized representational drawing and pictures generallly. We then try to relate these theories of pictures and picture perception to the main theoretical approaches to children's drawing.

In Chapter 4, we consider the relatively neglected question of why children draw at all. One of the hypotheses considered, for example, is the suggestion that children may find it satisfying in their drawing to exercise control over events in a way which may be impossible for them in real life. More generally, our discussion considers drawing as a form of solitary play as well as a social activity subject to social influences.

In Chapters 5 and 6, we cover the areas which have seen the most rapid and dramatic progress in knowledge and understanding in recent years. The questions addressed concern first, the important ways in which the processes involved in making a drawing can influence the finished product; and second, the different kinds of information that children present in their drawings. Our better understanding of the drawing process and new research suggest that children's drawings are far more sophisticated and convey far more information than had often been claimed in the past. An awareness of the role of the drawing process is essential for valid and useful interpretations of cognitive, motivational and emotional factors in drawing.

In Chapter 7 we apply these insights to ask whether or not children's drawings can give a reliable indication of their emotional state and personality, and how we can be sure that we have interpreted the indications correctly. In Chapter 8 we describe drawing development beyond childhood and consider some cases of exceptional drawing ability. In particular, we describe the amazing ability of some autistic children to produce photographically realistic pictures. In Chapter 9 we consider the striking similarity between some examples of modern art, primitive art and young children's spontaneous drawings. We then consider children's sensitivity to aesthetic and expressive aspects of drawing and discuss whether or not children's drawing can be considered as art. Chapter 10 concludes the book with some speculations about future directions in the study of children's drawing.

Illustrations

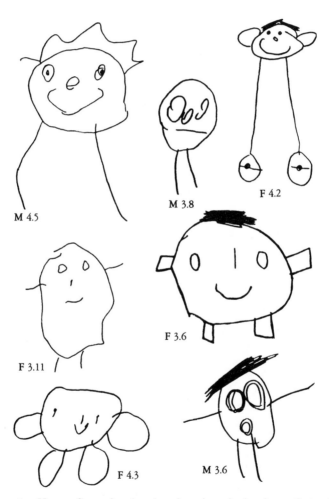

Figure 1: Human figure drawings based on the tadpole schema. Sex and age of drawer are indicated by each figure (M = boys, F = girls; age in years and months). Note that legs are portrayed with greater frequency than arms.

a. F 3.7

a. F 5.5

b. F 4.7

b. F 3.8

b. F 6.0

c. F 7.3

c. F 4.2

Figure 2: Human figure drawing based on the conventional schema in which a separate head and trunk are shown. *2.a*: Note the characteristic exaggeration of the head and the omission of the arms. *2.b*: Note the inappropriate placement of the arms at the side of the head. *2.c*: Note the alignment of the trunk and legs perpendicular to the axis of the eyes which have been drawn tilted with respect to the paper.

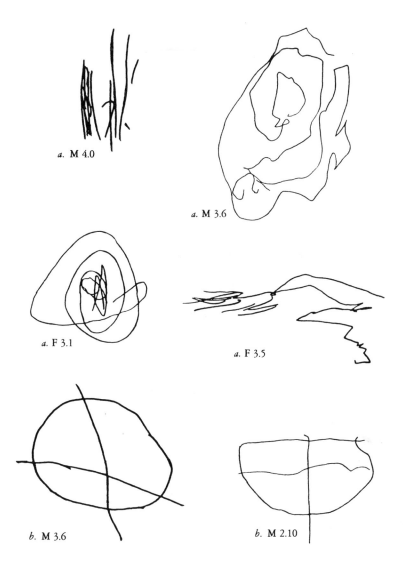

a. M 4.0

a. M 3.6

a. F 3.1

a. F 3.5

b. M 3.6

b. M 2.10

Figure 3: Scribbles and patterns drawn by two- to four-year-old children.
3.a: Scribbles. *3.b*: Mandalas.

8

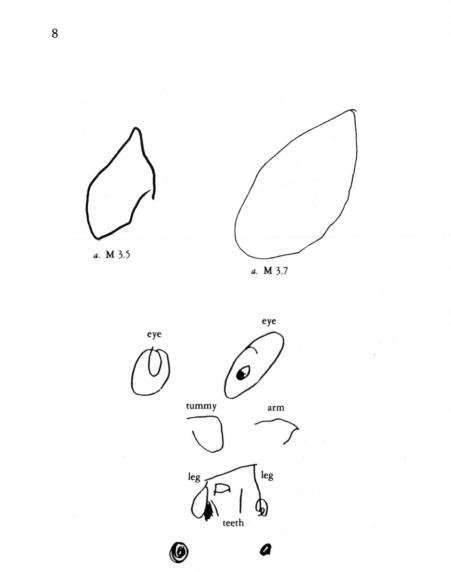

Figure 4: Drawings by three-year-old children. *4.a*: Primordial circles. *4.b*: Human figure drawing displaying synthetic incapability.

a. F 6.10

a. F 6.10

b. M 5.10

b. F 6.11

b. M 4.5

Figure 5: Transparency drawings. *5.a*: Fly in a spider's stomach and baby in a womb. *5.b*: Non-occlusion of the collar around the dog's neck, and the legs behind the horse and the table.

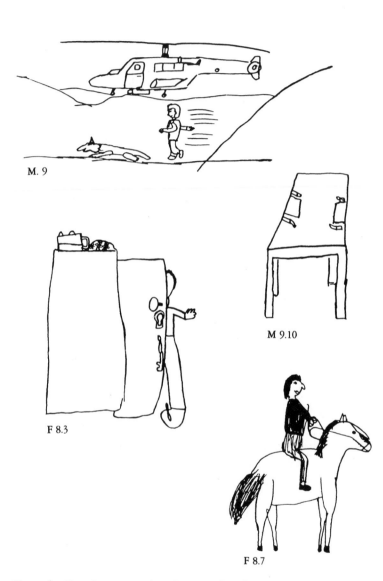

M. 9

M 9.10

F 8.3

F 8.7

Figure 6: Drawings presenting view-specific information by eight- and nine-year-old children.

a. M 4.6

b. M 4.3

c. M 5.1

Figure 7: Drawings of a man and a dog made by four- and five-year-old children. Regardless of the schema employed, the men are drawn taller than the dogs. 7.*a*: Note the use of a conventional schema for the man and a tadpole schema for the dog. 7.*b* and 7.*c*: Note the evolution of a profile schema for the dog.

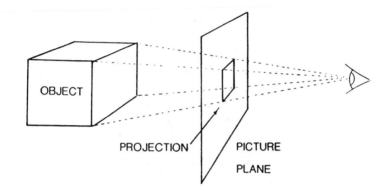

OBJECT

PROJECTION

PICTURE
PLANE

Figure 8:   Projection onto a picture plane.

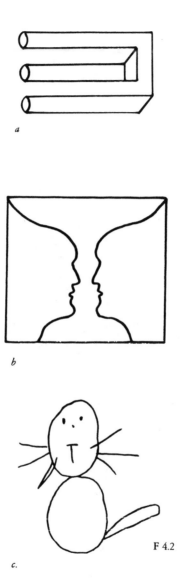

a

b

F 4.2

c.

Figure 9.a: An impossible object: the Devil's tuning fork. *9.b*: Rubin's figure and ground phenomenon (either the vase or the two faces can readily be perceived as the figure with the other possibility becoming the background). *9.c*: A schematic cat drawn by a four-year-old child.

14

a. M 6.2   *a.* F 6.7   *a.* F 4.11

b. M 5.6   *b.* M 4.9   *b.* F 6.4

c. F 6.2   *c.* M 7.11   *c.* F 6.1

Figure 10: Human figure drawings by four- to eight-year-old children.
10.*a*: Figures constructed out of simple shapes. 10.*b*: Figures involving a
threaded contour. 10.*c*: Figures combining constructed and threaded elements.

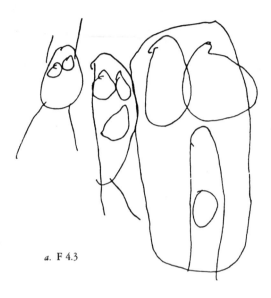

a. F 4.3

b. M 4.6

Figure 11.a: A four-year-old child's drawing of a house, a man and a dog, all based on the same schema. *11.b:* A four-year-old child's drawing of a house and a man. Note the exaggeration of the size of the man relative to the house and to the door.

M 4.1

F 5.10

M 4.6

F 5.6

Figure 12: Examples of human figure drawings based on the conventional schema made by four- and five-year-old children.

a. 7.6 (approx.)

b. 4.6 (approx.)

c. 7.6 (approx.)

Figure 13: In each pair of drawings the man on the left was elicited without special instructions. In *13.a* the child was asked to draw a man so as to show his teeth; in *13.b* details of the jacket were requested; and in *13.c* a back view was requested so that the face could not be seen. Note the consequent changes in relative sizes of head and trunk to accommodate the requested details.

F 6.6

F 7.9

F 9.0

Figure 14:   Competition for space. Note the various solutions to the conflict for space between the arms and the hair.

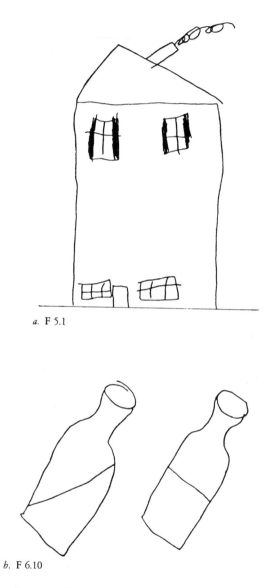

a. F 5.1

b. F 6.10

Figure 15: Common alignment errors. *15.a*: Chi·ıney on a house roof.
15.b: Surface of liquid in a beaker.

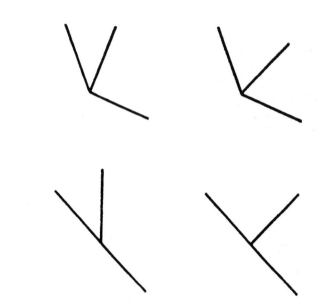

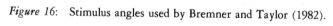

Figure 16: Stimulus angles used by Bremner and Taylor (1982).

F 9.0

F 5.6

M 10.4

F 6.0

F 5.6

Figure 17: Drawings of car, fish, horse, man and house in their canonical orientations.

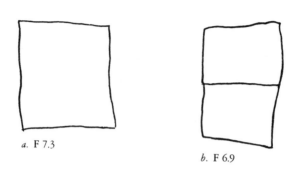

a. F 7.3

b. F 6.9

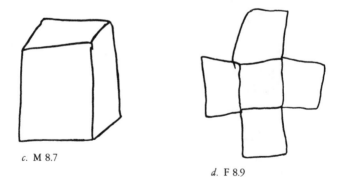

c. M 8.7

d. F 8.9

Figure 18: Children's drawings of a cube.

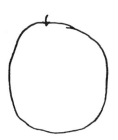

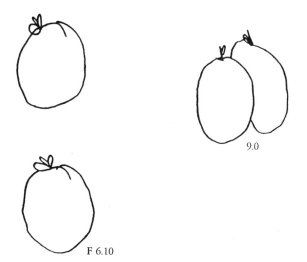

Figure 19: Children's drawings of one apple behind another.

F 10.0

F 9.8

F 11.2

Figure 20:   Drawings of a woman by nine- to eleven-year-old girls. Note the emphasis on the mouth.

F 10.9

F 8.8

F 9.10

Figure 21: Human figure drawings by eight- to eleven-year-old children. Note that the body is drawn in front view and the head in profile.

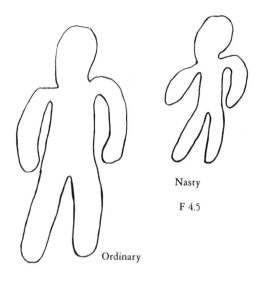

Nasty

F 4.5

Ordinary

Figure 22:   Copied drawings of an outline characterized as ordinary or nasty.

Figure 23: Photographically realistic and highly detailed drawing by Stephen Wiltshire, aged ten years.

1 History and theoretical overview

The modern study of children's drawings dates from the late nineteenth century. Much of the early research into children's drawing has been comprehensively reviewed by Harris (1963) and the interested reader is referred to his account for details. For present purposes it will be sufficient to outline several distinct periods in the history of research into children's drawing, each associated with a particular theoretical approach.

Developmental approaches

From about 1885 to the 1920s there was widespread interest in establishing a taxonomy of children's art. Considerable efforts were made in several different countries to collect children's spontaneous drawings and to describe and catalogue them. Many early investigators seem to have assumed that, in some sense, a child's drawing is a copy of an image in the child's mind and, therefore, that a child's drawings provide a "window" into his/her thoughts and feelings. The large numbers of drawings thus collected were inspected and classified, often in relation to the gender or cultural background of the drawer. In several studies the popularity of different drawing topics was recorded and in some cases an attempt was made to construct an objective scoring system for describing the drawings (e.g. Schuyten, 1904).

Perhaps the most important achievement of the early studies, however, was that they provided a basis for the classification of children's drawings into developmental sequences. Three investigators, in particular, made important contributions towards the identification of such sequences in children's drawing. Kerschensteiner (1905) studied thousands of drawings made by German schoolchildren and arrived at three broad categories which represented a rough age sequence: schematic drawings, drawings in terms of visual appearance and drawings that attempt representations of three-dimensional space. Rouma (1913) studied the drawings made by schoolchildren over a period of time and distinguished ten stages in the development of drawings of the human figure. Perhaps, however, the most significant of these early classifications was that proposed by Luquet (1913, 1927); this classification of five stages of development has been important, partly because it embodied a unifying theory and partly because of its influence on the subsequent work of Piaget.

Luquet assumed that children's drawings were based on an internal mental model (Piaget's term is 'mental image'). Luquet (and subsequently Piaget), however, also postulated that children's drawings were essentially realistic in intention; that is to say, the drawer intended to produce a recognizable and realistic representation of some object. Luquet was aware that several factors (including graphic skill and interpretation) could influence the translation of the internal model into the finished drawing. Accordingly, his proposed sequence of drawing development postulated developmental stages in organizational and graphic skills as well as in the child's realistic intentions (for details, see Chapter 2).

Against the background of developmental stages proposed by Luquet (and others), Florence Goodenough in 1926 published her book on the measurement of intelligence by drawings. This work, and a subsequent revision and extension by Harris (1963), established and shaped a long tradition of using drawings to assess intellectual development. The main product of this work was the "draw-a-man" test, in which a child's drawing of the human figure is assessed by crediting each feature included on the figure to give a score known as the Goodenough Intelligence Quotient. The principal underlying assumption is that a child's drawing is directly expressive of his/her concept of the topic concerned. The reliability of the "draw-a-man" test is good when testers are restricted to one drawing per child. Reliability is much less impressive across different drawings from the same child, because children often spontaneously vary their drawings (see Chapter 2). The "draw-a-man" test is no longer regarded as a valid measure of intelligence (as assessed by other criteria), although it can be useful as a screening test for those of below-average intelligence (Scott, 1981). In practice, the test is most useful for individuals whose mental ages fall within the range of 3-10 years. Once drawing was no longer widely used to assess intelligence, it became a relatively neglected topic for study within developmental psychology. Part of the explanation for this neglect lies in the Piagetian theory which came to dominate developmental psychology. Piaget assigned to drawing a status halfway between that of symbolic play and mental images (see Chapter 4). While Piaget sometimes used children's drawings to illustrate his theory (especially those aspects concerned with the representation of space), studies of drawings were never central to the development of his theory, nor did they offer crucial tests of his propositions. Consequently, neither Piaget nor subsequent investigators influenced by his theories devoted much attention to children's drawings. By the 1970s, many contemporary textbooks on cognitive development and child psychology scarcely mentioned children's drawing.

Clinical-projective approaches

From 1940 onwards, another interest in children's drawing began to flourish, based on the assumption that children project their emotions and motives into their drawings. This use of drawing to assess personality and psychological adjustment formed part of a wider use of projective methods in clinical psychology and psychiatry. As with other projective methods, such as the Rorschach ink-blot test, the interpretive use of drawings for personality assessment has often relied more on intuitive and subjective impressions that on scientific analysis. Consequently, a coherent and validated system for the assessment of emotional expression in drawings has been slow to emerge (see Chapter 7). For the present, we can note a fundamental similarity between the Goodenough-Harris assumption, that drawings were directly expressive of concepts, and the clinicians' beliefs, that drawings were directly expressive of emotional states. As Freeman (1972) put it, both these approaches were united in their consideration only of the surface structure of the finished drawing, regardless of the processes by which children construct their drawings.

Artistic approaches

From the end of the nineteenth century some educators began to believe that artistic expression could play a crucial role in children's development and education. An early influence on this emerging tradition was Cizek in Vienna. Later proponents in Europe have included Hanns and Michaela Strauss of the Waldorf and Rudolph Steiner Schools Fellowships (see Strauss, 1978). Another crucial figure in this tradition was Viktor Lowenfeld. Lowenfeld believed that individual self-expression in art is essential for healthy emotional and personal development – a principle that is based partly on psychoanalytic ideas, but also on Lowenfeld's experiences of the rise of authoritarianism under the Nazis and of the German occupation of Austria in 1938 (see Efland, 1976). These experiences led Lowenfeld to stress the importance of encouraging free and spontaneous self-expression in art and in education. On emigrating from Europe, Lowenfeld was powerfully influential in translating this art education tradition to North America (Lowenfeld, 1947).

Another significant artistic approach to drawing is that of Rudolph Arnheim and his many followers (e.g. Kellogg, 1970; Goodnow, 1977; Gardner, 1980). In his book *Art and Visual Perception*, Arnheim (1956) has provided the most psychologically sophisticated and currently best-known application of Gestalt perceptual psychology to art generally and to children's drawing in particular. Arnheim's theory of art is notable because it provides one of the most comprehensive theoretical accounts of children's drawing, incorporating perceptual, emotional-expressive and cognitive-developmental considerations within a unifying framework. In particular, Arnheim's work yielded structural descriptions of children's drawings in terms of the Gestalt principles of perceptual organization. In a later work, Arnheim (1969) has also made a plea for greater emphasis on visual thinking in our culture and education (see also Kellogg, 1970; Goodnow, 1977).

In some ways these artistic-expressive traditions can be seen as educational applications of the clinical notion that children will project their emotional, perceptual and intellectual experiences into their drawings. The important additional principle proposed by Strauss, Lowenfeld and other educationalists is that encouraging spontaneous self-expression in art promotes cognitive development and personal growth. The logical development of this view is that drawing (and other artistic activity) could play an important role both in therapy and in education. The underlying psychological theorizing may be critized for its vagueness. Nevertheless, Lowenfeld and others in this tradition have suggested a wealth of ideas and principles which have been a significant influence on art education and art therapy in Western Europe and North America for the past fifty years.

Process approaches

All the theoretical approaches described so far largely consider only the surface structure of children's drawings. As a consequence, all these theoretical approaches neglected the possible role of the process of constructing the drawing in determining the final structure of a picture. Several authorities, for example, have commented that Piaget's theory of children's drawing was seriously inadequate: in effect, he simply incorporated Luquet's theory into his own more general theory of cognitive development (see Freeman, 1972, 1980; Selfe, 1983). Piaget adopted from Luquet the proposition that a drawing is an attempt to represent the real world and is based on a mental image (Piaget and Inhelder, 1969). What Piaget's theory does not adequately encompass are the organizational and procedural problems faced by a child trying to make a drawing. Lack of consideration for those performance factors involved in translating conceptual knowledge (or a mental image) into a recognizable representation on paper frequently led Piaget to underestimate children's knowledge. Freeman (1980) has presented many examples of the substantial effects performance biases and planning difficulties can have on the final form of a finished drawing. Piagetian theory, the Goodenough-Harris approach to intellectual assessment and clinical-projective analyses of drawing were all alike in their failure to consider adequately the process of making a drawing as well as the structure of the finished product.

It would be hard to overstate the consequences of these earlier failures to take account of the drawing process. Consideration of only the surface structure of drawings may lead to the neglect of important differences in drawing procedures. A disproportionately large head in a child's drawing of a person, for example, could signify that the child considers the head and face to be important; alternatively, it could signify that the child has not yet solved the planning problem of leaving enough space on the paper for the body when the head is drawn first (see Chapter 5). This is an empirical question, but one with profound implications for the interpretation of drawings for what they can reveal about hypothesized representational structures in the mind or about emotional and perceptual experience. It may be, for example, that better understanding of the process factors may allow more valid and reliable interpretations of drawings as expressions of personality and emotional states.

The shift from viewing drawings as a "print-out" of mental contents to considering them as constructions whose final form depends crucially on the procedures used to produce them has been one of the most important recent developments in the study of children's drawing. Indeed, so fundamental is this change in our approach to children's drawing that its consequences may yet restore children's art to a central position in child cognitive psychology. Although many authorities now recognize the importance of considering the process of constructing a drawing, to date the most extensive and coherent analysis of the production process has been offered by Freeman (1980). The strategies used by children in making drawings are of interest not only because they allow us to make a more satisfactory analysis of children's art, but also because they open up the possibility of progress in understanding the development of planning and organizing skills in general.

Summary

To some extent, then, this brief and selective history allows us to identify some of the reasons why anyone should ever want to study children's drawing. There are aesthetic reasons – because the drawings are often charming and appealing in themselves. There are educational reasons – because the development of graphic art may teach important skills of visual thinking as well as beneficial expressive skills. There are clinical reasons – because drawings may be useful in personality assessment or in the diagnosis of psychological disorder. Furthermore, there may be a clinical therapeutic value in the development of means of emotional expression in art therapy. Finally, we find that analysis of the construction process in making a drawing may contribute to developmental and cognitive psychology for what it tells us about strategies of representation and the presentation of information.

2 Characteristics of children's drawing

In Chapter 1 we identified some of the main historical landmarks in the study of children's drawing. This second chapter is also aimed at helping readers new to the subject area by briefly describing the general character of children's drawing at different ages. Most studies of children's drawing which have produced large amounts of data (e.g. Goodenough, 1926; Kellogg, 1970) were cross-sectional and there have been relatively few longitudinal studies of individual children developing their drawing skills (but see Luquet, 1913; Fenson, 1985). Nevertheless, these cross-sectional studies have provided an empirical foundation for the categorization of children's drawings into a series of distinct stages. Most of these early studies were also primarily concerned only with descriptions of the finished drawing product. Although the processes involved in constructing a drawing may crucially influence the final form of a drawing (Freeman, 1972, 1980), these will be considered in detail later in this book (see Chapter 5).

Broadly speaking, as children grow older their drawings become more detailed, better proportioned and more realistic (see Harris, 1963). There are, however, some striking and distinctive features which characterize the drawings often made by children at each stage in their drawing development.

Classification of developmental stages

Eighteen months to two-and-a-half years
Children usually begin to make marks on paper from the age of about eighteen months onwards. According to most investigators, these scribbles are not aimless and uncoordinated movements, but demonstrate awareness of pattern and increasing eye–hand co-ordination. Figure 3a. shows some examples of

scribbles made by such young children. In 8,000 or so children's drawings collected over many years of research, Kellogg (1970) has distinguished twenty basic types of scribble, in addition to seventeen placement patterns (these are related to the location of marks on the paper).

Kellogg has reported, for example, that children will position their scribbles on the page to achieve a degree of visual balance or will position one scribble on top of an earlier one. Interestingly, Morris (1967) has reported rather similar patterns in paintings made by chimpanzees provided with paints and paper. Both chimpanzees and children seem to find the production of scribbles quite absorbing (Chapter 4), and adults often find the resulting patterns and shapes aesthetically pleasing (Chapter 9).

In general, investigators have agreed that many of these early scribbles are not intended to be representations of anything. Both Luquet and Piaget, for example, considered early scribbles to be pure play and exercise (Piaget and Inhelder, 1969). Arnheim (1956) took a similar view: he suggested that these first scribbles are not "representations" but "presentations" in which the "motor impulse" strongly dominates. The child moves his/her arm in a regular rhythmic motion around the page, but at the same time s/he is interested in the marks that appear on the paper.

There comes a point, however, when children start to interpret their scribbles as pictures. Luquet (1913, 1927), who extensively studied the drawings of his daughter, identified this stage as that of "fortuitous realism". Typically, children do not announce their intentions before starting to draw; rather they interpret their drawing after its completion. Arnheim (1956) has noted that the first enclosed form made by children - the "primordial circle" - appears to be able to stand for almost any object from the child's environment (see Figure 4.a). Arnheim claims that the circle is the simplest visual pattern for young children and one for which they not only have a perceptual preference, but which also allows for endless experimentation. Arnheim also considered that the motor pleasure which children derive from drawing continues to be important even after their drawings become recognizable as representations. While Arnheim may well be correct in this, we should note that he offered little independent verification for these claims (see Chapter 4).

Two-and-a-half years to five years

It becomes more obvious that, from the age of about two-and-a-half years, children see their drawings as representations of something. Intentions are sometimes declared before the drawing is started and the meaning of the drawing is no longer left unexplained until after its completion. There is, however, still an element of opportunism in children's interpretation of their drawings. Luquet noted that children at this stage in their development often depart from their initial declared intention if the drawing turns out to look like something else. Indeed, the interpretations such young children place on their drawings may often change over time. Freeman (1987) provides further detailed discussion of this flexibility in children's interpretations of their drawing.

Scribbles now become more easily recognizable by others and gradually more shapes are rehearsed in greater numbers on the same sheet of paper. Kellogg (1970) has produced a widely-known and detailed analysis of the shapes and patterns that may be found in children's drawing. Although Kellogg studied a large number of drawings, we should warn that her research was unsystematic and we cannot be certain that her idealized progressions and orders of complexity really are representative of the drawing development of individual children.

According to Kellogg, undifferentiated and irregular forms gradually become identifiable as circles, squares, triangles and crosses. These shapes, which are all drawn in outline form, are often superimposed one on another, thus becoming what Kellogg (1970) has called "combines". Larger numbers of scribbles in close proximity to each other she terms "aggregates". A frequently occurring example of a combine at this drawing stage, according to Kellogg, is a "mandala" – a cross superimposed on a circle – which she claims is a "good" shape, that is, one inherently pleasing to children (see Figure 3.b). Kellogg believes that children's preference for this shape shows their search for order, harmony and overall balance in their drawings. There is, however, little independent evidence that children do find such shapes satisfying other than the observation that the shapes sometimes appear in their drawings (see Chapters 4 and 9).

Other important shapes in the child's drawings, according to Kellogg, are suns, circles and radials. It is, for example, from the circle, which has enormous graphic potential, that the first representations of the human figure finally emerge (see also Britsch, 1926; Schaefer-Simmern, 1948; Arnheim, 1956). The shapes characteristic of this "pre-representational stage" are often incorporated in later representational drawings (see Arnheim, 1956; Winner, 1982). The shape of a sun, for example, may later also be drawn as a hand in a human figure drawing.

Children of three-and-a-half years of age, who have started to make representational drawings, will sometimes fail to co-ordinate the parts of a drawing. They may, for example, draw the eyes or the "tummy" outside the outline of the rest of the body (see Figure 4.b). Luquet (1913) suggested that this phenomenon, described as "synthetic incapability" by Freeman (1980), was characteristic of what he has called the stage of "failed realism". Synthetic incapability is not due to a false relationship between the elements in the drawing but, rather, to an absence of a relationship between these elements (see Freeman, 1972).

Beyond the age of about three-and-a-half years, children start to bring the details of a drawing into relationship with each other. Many of their drawings at this stage seem to be based on simple formulas or schemata (Lowenfeld, 1947). At this stage, for example, a typical drawing of a human figure consists of a circle for the head (or a combined head and trunk) and two dangling lines for legs. Marks within the circle may be used to signify facial details, such as eyes and mouth. Such "tadpole" figures, as they are often called, are simple in form, but often appear to adults to be very expressive and aesthetically interesting (but see Chapter 9). Several examples of tadpole figures are presented in Figure 1. Note that only a few shapes (mainly circles) are used to make these drawings. Each kind of shape can come to stand for almost anything – circles, for example, are often used to signify head, body, eyes, hand or nose. Indeed, the tadpole schema may itself be used for a variety of purposes, signifying different people or even animals as the occasion demands.

These schematic drawings sometimes appear to function more as symbols than as attempts to represent accurately the appearance of the topic depicted. Children who live in blocks of flats have, for example, been observed to make stylized drawings of houses with gabled roofs and smoking chimneys when asked to draw their own homes. The term "symbolic realism" is sometimes used to describe the representational character of drawings of this kind (Barrett and Light, 1976).

Five years to eight years

In general, as children get older their drawings become increasingly realistic. Drawings made by children aged five to seven years, however, sometimes still contain elements which the child knows to exist, even though they cannot normally be seen. The result is a so-called "transparency" or "X-ray" drawing, which is characteristic of what Luquet has termed the stage of "intellectual realism". Freeman (1980) has distinguished between two types of X-ray drawing. First, there are the drawings in which something is depicted that is usually never visible in the real world – for example, a baby may be shown in the mother's womb or a fly in a spider's stomach (see Figure 5.a). In this type of drawing, it seems clear that the child intended to show the normally hidden contents of the stomach. In the second type of transparency the child fails to show occlusion of something that is normally hidden behind a nearer object. Children at this stage may, for example, draw a man on horseback so that the normally hidden far leg of the rider can be seen through the body of a horse (see Figure 5.b).

In other respects, drawings by children at this stage are increasingly visually realistic in terms of scaling and detail. At this stage, their human figure drawings have progressed beyond the tadpole schema and now depict a separate head and trunk. Additional details, such as hands, fingers and clothing, are increasingly likely to be portrayed.

Eight years to adolescence

Children of eight years and older often attempt to portray depth in their drawings, not only in individual objects but also as a relationship between objects. Children now begin to draw from a particular viewpoint (see Figure 6) and proportions and relationships are worked out accordingly. This latter stage in drawing development has been termed "visual realism" by Luquet. Children's drawings, then, appear to progress, becoming more visually realistic (according to conventional Western standards) as the child grows older.

The free drawings of older children, aged nine or ten years, also gradually become more conventional in style. Cartoon figures and comic-strip figures are now drawn regularly. The drawings show less variability and less idiosyncrasy. Children at this stage often appear to become dissatisfied with their drawing and no longer pursue this activity, largely, it is claimed, because of their inability to achieve the effects they desire in their drawing. Those children who do continue to draw, either as a result of encouragement from others or through self-education, often seem to develop their own imagery, characters and caricatures, thereby maintaining a certain freedom in their expression (Gardner, 1980).

Generally speaking, drawing is not considered to be a central part of the school curriculum for older children in most Western countries. According to Arnheim (1969), a common result is the neglect of drawing by older children and its replacement by language as a medium for self-expression. Gardner (1980) has suggested that the increasing visual realism of older children's drawing may also make it a less satisfactory medium for the expression of their feelings. A problem with many of these claims and assertions, however, is that they are seldom supported by systematically collected data.

Universal stages of drawing development?

Although the majority of studies reviewed in this chapter have only been concerned with European and North American children, there do seem to be many similarities in the drawing development of children from different cultures, at least up to the age of seven or eight years. Some investigators, such as Kellogg (1970), have argued that there is a universal pattern of development in children's drawings and art. Others, such as Alland (1983), have maintained that such claims are exaggerated, and Deregowski (1980) has suggested that the drawing of children reared away from Western influences may develop in quite different ways.

Alland (1983) makes the interesting suggestion that children in different cultures may differ not only in details of drawing style, but also in the basic strategies used to construct their drawings (cf. Freeman, 1980). Thus, for example, a particular shape may occur frequently in drawings made by children from a particular culture, not because it is aesthetically pleasing to those children, but because it is a by-product of a culturally-determined drawing strategy. Only when the causes of cross-cultural differences in drawing have been identified can we establish, according to Alland, whether or not there are patterns and shapes with universal aesthetic appeal. Alland also claimed that some older children, reared in a culture without a tradition of representational drawing, can begin to draw immediately in a representational way once given the opportunity. Such an achievement, of course, cannot be based on the earlier scribbling stages that Kellogg claimed to be necessary precursors to the emergence of representational drawing (see report by Gardner, 1980).

There is, of course, a problem with any classification into stages in that it tends to obscure the continuities in development. With regard to drawing, there does not appear to be a fixed relationship between a child's age and the stages s/he has achieved in his/her drawings. Drawing typical of earlier stages often persists even when more developed strategies have been attained. Take, for example, the achievement of a separate head and trunk in figure drawing. Children who have mastered this skill may still revert to drawing tadpole figures, even in the same picture. Figure 7a, for example, shows a tadpole dog, even though the child has drawn a separate body in the picture of a man.

Wilson and Wilson (1977) record a dramatic illustration that there need be no fixed relation between age and stage of drawing development. These authors were working with elderly Jewish immigrants to the United States from Poland and Hungary. This group had not, apparently, made any drawings since early childhood, and when asked to draw and paint many of them produced tadpole figures comparable to those normally produced by four-year-olds. Wilson and Wilson argue that practice at drawing and exposure to other people's drawings are necessary for what we have described as normal drawing development.

Summary

Generally, children's drawings can be classified into five stages, starting with the scribbling stage at about eighteen months to two years. Gradually, designs emerge at about two to three years that cannot quite be called representational until the child is about three to four years old, when figures based on the tadpole schema emerge. These drawings become more coherent as the children become older. During the stage of intellectual realism children often make X-ray drawings. It is not until the child is about eight years old that visually realistic drawings start to appear.

3 What is a drawing?

In the last two chapters we have looked at the background to the study of children's drawing and described some important features of children's drawing development. It is now time to address the fundamental question of what a drawing is. Some drawings amount only to scribbles or decorative patterns that are relatively easy to define and describe. However, most children brought up under Western influences make drawings that are pictures, that is, they are representations of something. In most cases, therefore, the problem of defining what a drawing is becomes one of defining what a picture is. This turns out to be a surprisingly difficult matter, and one which has seldom been explicitly addressed by psychologists studying children's drawing (but see Arnheim, 1956; Selfe, 1983). Inevitably, however, all theories of children's drawing make assumptions about the nature of pictures and we think it important to clarify these assumptions and discuss their implications.

Although pictures are a common part of our everyday life, it is not at all easy to produce a satisfactory definition of what a picture is:

nothing even approximating a science of depiction exists. What artists, critics, and philosophers of art have to say about pictures has little in common with what photographers, opticists, and geometers have to say about them. They do not seem to be talking about the same topic. No one seems to know what a picture *is*. (Gibson, 1979, p.270)

In a limited way, it is obvious that a picture is a series of marks on a flat surface. The problems of definition and explanation concern the way in which those marks represent something else: the subject of the picture. A major issue dividing theories of pictures concerns the relation between perception of a picture and natural perception of the real world. We consider next some of these theories of pictures and their associated theories of visual perception.

Pictures as symbols

We start our discussion with the extreme position that pictures are a symbolic and arbitrary code and that "seeing" a picture need bear no specific relation at all to visual perception of the world. A leading proponent of this argument, Goodman (1976), has asserted that the marks which make a picture are "read" as symbols in a language. It is quite unnecessary, he claims, for there to be any physical resemblance between a graphic symbol and the topic depicted:

The plain fact is that a picture, to represent an object, must be a symbol for it, stand for it, refer to it; and that no degree of resemblance is sufficient to establish the requisite relationship of reference. Nor is resemblance *necessary* for reference; almost anything may stand for almost anything else. A picture that represents – like a passage that describes – an object refers to and, more particularly, denotes it. Denotation is the core of representation and is independent of resemblance. (Goodman, 1976, p. 5)

This argument suggests, for example, that a picture of a dog and the word "dog" are both symbols and there need be no physical similarity between the picture of a dog and the appearance of a real dog. If a picture of a dog looks convincingly realistic to us, it is simply a matter of habit: we have learned to interpret pictures made in a given artistic style much as we have learned the meanings of words of the English language. As a general theory this proposal is clearly incorrect. The main objection to it is the good evidence that no special learning is required for people to be able to recognize the topics of pictures. In their classic study, Hochberg and Brooks (1962) found that a nineteen-month-old child with no prior experience of object identification in pictures was as accurate in identifying familiar objects from line drawings as in identifying the objects themselves. No prior learning of the conventions of pictorial labels, as required by Goodman's theory, could have taken place. Further evidence comes from cross-cultural studies which have often found that the recognition of objects in pictures (line drawings as well as photographs) often seems to be immediate, and therefore unlearned, in cultures and societies where pictures were rare or unknown (see reviews by Hagen and Jones, 1978; Jones and Hagen, 1980). It has also been found that some animals can recognize the topics of pictures and photographs, also presumably without any prior learning of the meaning of pictorial symbols (for a review see Cabe, 1980). The evidence is clear, therefore, that many pictures present information which has enough in common with that provided by the perception of the real world for the immediate identification of the object depicted.

Although we must reject the idea that pictures are nothing more than a conventional, symbolic code, we should note that some pictorial features may have a predominantly conventional meaning in Goodman's sense. It appears from the evidence of cross-cultural studies, for example, that pictorial devices for indicating motion (or impact or pain) are merely conventional in our Western culture, and are often misinterpreted by people from other cultures (see Friedman and Stevenson, 1980).

Furthermore, apart from being representations of objects, pictures can also be expressions of ideas, feelings and emotions. Such intangibles cannot be directly perceived in reality, and a symbol for an idea cannot literally reproduce the appearance of an idea in the same way that a picture can seem to copy the appearance of an object. It may be that an analysis of pictures as symbols, with interpretations determined partly by convention, is more relevant to the expression of ideas and feelings than to the portrayal of appearances. Of the theoretical approaches described in Chapter 1, only some of the artistic approaches gave significant consideration to the possibility that children might learn to draw in ways that give symbolic expression to their feelings about the topic portrayed (see Arnheim, 1969; Lowenfeld, 1947). We discuss this possibility further in Chapters 5, 7 and 9.

Perceptual theories of pictures

Many theorists have suggested that the normal, spontaneous recognition of pictures is not just a well-practised act of interpretation but is based on a physical resemblance between a picture and its topic. In one sense a picture copies the appearance of its subject and perceiving a picture involves processes related to those involved in perceiving the object itself. It follows, therefore, that our conception of pictures and picture perception depends on what we think visual perception of the real world involves. Hagen (1980a) classifies perceptual theories as:

1. Gibsonian ecological theories, which suggest that perception consists of detecting the meaningful structures which already exist in the external visual world,
2. constructivist theories, which suggest that perception consists of constructing perceptual meaning according to our past experience out of an essentially ambiguous visual input to the eye, and
3. Gestalt theories, which suggest that perception consists of structuring visual input according to the Gestalt laws of perceptual organization.

Each of these theories of perception is associated with a particular theory of picture perception; and each theory of picture perception in turn is associated with some implications for picture production. We shall consider each theory in turn.

Ecological theories I:
perspective-projection theories of picture perception
One influential and long-established version of ecological theory considers visual perception to be the extraction of information from the "picture'" produced by visual input on the retina of the eye. This form of ecological theory is associated with the early work of James Gibson (e.g. Gibson, 1950), but many other theorists have also favoured this approach (e.g. Kennedy, 1974; Hagen, 1976; Haber, 1980). Theories of this type start to analyse vision by considering the perception of a

static, "frozen" momentary image on the retina. Gibson (1950) stressed how gradients of optical texture can provide sufficient information to specify the relative sizes, shapes, orientations and positions of objects located on a plane or depicted on a flat surface. Such an approach has sometimes been called "the picture theory of perception" (Costall, 1985) or "perspectivism" (Hagen, 1980b).

The perspective-projection theory of vision has little trouble in explaining picture perception. According to Haber (1980), for example, a picture of a scene provides much of the same visual stimulation as looking at a scene through a window. In other words, a convincing picture presents to the eye much the same pattern of visual stimulation (contours and texture gradients, for example) as a real object or scene.

By stressing the common features of picture perception and perception of the real world, this model raises the question of how light "rays" to the eye from a particular three-dimensional scene can be reproduced by a pattern of marks on the two-dimensional surface of a picture. This account of picture perception, therefore, assigns special significance to the discovery/invention by Renaissance artists of the rules and techniques of artificial perspective – a technique for constructing a projection of a real object onto the flat surface of a picture. The result is often described as a "perspective" picture (see Figure 8).

An important problem for all projective models of picture perception is that the projection of a scene in a picture is designed to be viewed from only one particular station point, that adopted by the camera or the artist when the scene was photographed or painted. As soon as the viewer of the picture moves away from that original station point then the projections of the shapes in the picture become distorted. It is easy to confirm from one's own experience, however, that pictures do not appear distorted even when viewed from very extreme angles. Pirenne (1970) suggested that our awareness of the picture surface enables us to determine what the correct station point should be, and automatically to compensate for any distortions in the pattern of projected light produced by an anomolous station point. Haber (1980) suggests that we may use similar unconscious compensation to discount the fact that some of the presumed sources of depth information that operate in normal perception of the world, such as head and eye movements and binocular disparity, are not available in pictures.

Perspective-projective theory seems to be most useful for explaining very realistic artwork, such as *trompe l'oeil*, which can create such powerful three-dimensional effects that a skilfully-made picture can be mistaken for real, solid objects (Pirenne, 1970; Mackavey, 1980). The important point about the success of such *trompe l'oeil* artwork in this context is that it reminds us that natural perception and picture perception must, at least sometimes, have a great deal in common for such illusions to succeed.

A propos children's drawing, Arnheim (1956) has argued that a naïve form of the perspective-projection theory underlies the developmental theories of Goodenough and Harris, and even Piaget, as well as the clinical-projective theories of Machover and Koppitz. The relation of all these accounts of children's drawing to perspective-projection theory lies in their shared assumption that children's drawings are imperfect attempts to produce a picture that is a realistic copy of the topic portrayed. Put another way, all these theories, implicitly or explicitly, consider children's drawings as deviations from an ideal, visually correct, perspective projection.

Harris (1963), for example, had little to say explicitly about picture perception, but it is fundamental to his approach that a visually correct perspective projection be taken as the standard against which children's drawings should be assessed. He considered that it was children's conceptual or intellectual immaturity which constrained their drawings and which explained why they fell short of the ideal of a visually correct projection. Piaget made very similar assumptions about children's realistic intentions, but suggested that it was their immature conceptions of three-dimensional space which were chiefly responsible for their failures to achieve visually correct representations. The clinical-projective theories of Machover (1949) and Koppitz (1968) also took visually-correct perspective projections as a standard against which the effects of personality and emotional variables could be assessed. More recently, Willats (1977) has suggested that there is a developmental progression towards a perspective projection in children's attempts to represent depth information in their drawing.

There are, however, some major problems with perspective-projection theory as an account of children's drawing. First, most children and artistically untrained adults do not produce visually-correct projections in their drawings and commonly use alternative projection systems to the perspective projection we have been discussing (see Hagen, 1985). Much of children's drawing, indeed, seems best described as caricature (see Freeman, 1980, and Eng, 1931), in which salient features are overemphasized at the expense of visual realism.

Second, it is obvious that even the most accomplished line drawings reproduce only a small fraction of the stimuli presented by a real scene. According to perspective-projection theory, a picture becomes a recognizable representation because it copies the stimuli of a real scene. Consequently, line drawings such as caricatures which present very few of the stimuli of a real scene should be hard to recognize. In reality, however, these simplified line drawings are apparently easily recognized even by subjects with no prior experience of pictures (see the study by Hochberg and Brooks, 1962). Moreover, a caricature may sometimes be more easily recognized than a photograph of the same object. Ryan and Schwartz (1956) asked subjects to view various representations of a human hand, each presented for only a fraction of a second. They found that a drawing of a hand from a Mickey Mouse cartoon film was more readily recognized than a realistic photograph of a hand.

These results pose a serious problem for perspective-projection theory, both as a general account of picture perception and also as an account of the perception of children's drawings in particular. A theory which suggests that our perception of pictures depends on pictures copying the stimuli from a real scene predicts that non-realistic pictures should be difficult to interpret, or at least less easy to see than realistic ones. While we do not wish to claim that the topics of children's drawings are always instantly recognizable, they are usually easy to see yet, at the same time, quite obviously nothing like the stimulation arising from a real scene. The inability of perspective-projection theory to account for the ready perception of caricature pictures was largely overcome, however, in Gibson's later versions of his ecological theory of perception (Gibson, 1979).

Ecological theories II:
Gibson's invariant information theory of picture perception

In his later writings on perception and picture perception, James Gibson rejected his earlier approach to perception which "begins with the eye fixed and exposed to a momentary pattern of stimuli" (Gibson, 1979, p. 303). One major weakness of the perspective approach, according to Gibson, is that the fixed-viewing conditions, which it takes to be fundamental, scarcely ever occur in real life and present so much ambiguity that, in order to perceive the world at all, the perceiver must already know something of what the world is like. The perspective theory then has the awkward task of explaining how this knowledge of the world arose independently of vision. Gibson's alternative is an ecological theory of perception which emphasizes the interactions between perceivers and their environment.

Gibson (1979) proposed that it is fundamental to visual perception that the eye is constantly moving and, therefore, that the visual input to the eye is constantly changing. He argued that we extract information about the invariant structure of the world directly from the flowing and ever-changing pattern of ambient light. What we see, therefore, is the world as it is; without conscious effort we are programmed to detect its invariant structure embedded in the continuously changing visual input to our eyes.

Gibson proposed that a picture is "a surface so treated that it makes available an optic array of arrested structures with underlying invariants of structure" (Gibson, 1979, p. 272). A picture, therefore, presents the structural invariants of the topic portrayed. As such, a picture registers information, but it is "a surface that always specifies something other than what it is" (Gibson, 1979, p. 73).

Unlike perspective theories, therefore, Gibson did *not* consider that a picture can present the same pattern of visual stimulation as a real scene. Rather, he proposed, a picture makes available to the spectator the same kind of information normally abstracted from viewing a real scene - specifically, structural invariants. An exhaustive list and description of all such invariants has not yet been made, although Gibson (1979) made a beginning to this task. In making a picture, he argued, we arrange structural invariants on paper.

A consequence of his emphasis on a "moving eye" and the detection of invariants of structure is that children's drawings will always be primarily concerned with the general or usual appearance of things and not, in the first instance, with presenting the appearance of a scene from a particular station point. The latter, he argued, is a late and specialized development both in real perception and in art. It is true that many children's drawings could be reasonably considered in these terms. Many authors have stressed that children often make canonical drawings (Freeman, 1980) that provide a typical or "standard" view of the topic. A similar point is captured in the often quoted assertion that children draw what they know, not what they see.

There are, however, several problems with Gibson's conceptualization of pictures as frozen invariants of structure. As Arnheim (1971) has argued, there is much art in which the presentation of a particular view is fundamental. Furthermore, the significance of a painting of a cornfield (such as by Van Gogh) is not that it presents the structural invariants of any cornfield, but that it presents a particular (and personal) impression of a cornfield. Equally, the "invariant" theory of pictures does not seem to provide a very convincing account of the powerful impression of a three-dimensional scene from a particular station point created by the use of artificial perspective in *trompe l'oeil* pictures.

Pictures of "impossible" objects are also difficult for Gibson's theory. Most people are familiar with Escher's pictures of never-ending staircases or with such objects as the Devil's tuning fork (Figure 9.a). The point about such pictures is that while they can readily be seen and interpreted, the impossibilities portrayed have no real structure and, therefore, cannot possess structural invariants for the picture to present to the viewer. Some of the more bizarre but common features of children's early drawings present the same kind of difficulty for Gibson's theory as do pictures of impossible objects. Where are the invariants of structure, for example, in a human figure drawing which displays synthetic incapability? Elements of the drawing seem to be scattered at random on the page, yet the drawing may still be recognizable (see Figure 4.b).

Constructivist theories of picture perception

For most of us, our experience of visual perception is normally so immediate, so effortless and so convincing that it requires an effort of imagination to appreciate that any explanation might be required. Constructivist theories, however, are built on the observation that the stimulus input to the eye and the image it produces on the retina is often ambiguous and capable of several different perceptual interpretations. According to this approach, a perception is a perceptual hypothesis based on the incomplete evidence provided by the visual input to the eye.

Constructivist theories are similar to perspective-projection theories in that both take as fundamental to vision a static image formed on the retina of the eye. The approaches differ in their accounts of what is done with this visual input. Whereas a perspective approach holds that the perceiver extracts information from this visual input, a constructivist theory holds that the perceiver constructs an interpretation of the visual input.

An important part of the constructivist approach is the claim that our visual world is much less stable and definite than we might normally believe. Any stability that our perceptions possess is supplied by our interpretation, not by the visual input. That perception consists of constructing meaning out of disorder and often ambiguous sensations is often illustrated by examples of stimuli that can be organized into more than one perception (see Figure 9.b). Interestingly, most of the often quoted examples of stimuli generating these alternative perceptions consist of pictures rather than natural scenes. Questions of interest posed by a constructivist theory of perception concern how a perceiver constructs a perception of three-dimensional space out of the two-dimensional image on the retina of the eye (but see Gibson, 1979) and how momentary variations in the stimuli impinging on the eye are organized into perceptions of a relatively stable world. Thus, much research within this tradition has been concerned with the phenomena of size constancy and depth perception, and the illusions which result when perceptual interpretive mechanisms are triggered inappropriately.

Classic examples of the inappropriate triggering of these organizational mechanisms are the impossible objects such as the Devil's tuning fork (see Figure 9.a). Such figures appear confusing, according to constructivist theorists, because we attempt to interpret the pattern of lines as representing a solid. No confusion would occur if we could induce ourselves to interpret the figure as a flat pattern (see, for example, Deregowski, 1980).

The constructivist tradition in visual perception can be traced back to Helmholtz (see Hagen, 1980b); more recent proponents include Hochberg (1978), Gregory (1966, 1970), Frisby (1979) and (arguably) Marr (1982). The application of a constructivist approach to picture perception and to art has been dominated by the work of Ernst Gombrich (1972, 1982). Constructivist theories account for the perception of pictures in the same way as they account for perception of the real world. Constructivist theories propose that natural perception consists of the interpretation of an image on the retina of the eye. Consequently, picture perception, which consists of the interpretation of an image on a piece of paper, can be explained using the same principles. According to Gombrich (e.g. Gombrich, 1971), the principal difference between a real scene and a picture of that scene is that the picture usually provides less stimulus material for the viewer to interpret.

In terms of a constructivist theory of perception, then, a drawing is a pattern of marks on paper which stimulates perceptual interpretations by the spectator. Gombrich's theory of picture making gives a central role to what he calls pictorial schemata. These schemata are techniques of depiction (such as the rules of linear perspective or the blurring of outlines to signal distance) or construction formulas (such as that in Figure 9.c to represent a cat). Schemata are essential for picture making: "without a medium and without a schema which can be molded and modified, no artist could imitate reality" (Gombrich, 1972, p. 126). Note, however, that in this constructivist theory the artist's schemata do not copy the appearance of a real scene in a picture, but merely suggest its appearance to the viewer.

The emphasis in constructivist theory on picture-making techniques is strikingly similar to process approaches to children's drawing which assert the crucial influence of the production process on the final form of a child's drawing. Gombrich has suggested that the history of art is largely the history of the invention/discovery of new schemata and graphic devices for making pictures. Similarly, Freeman (1980) has argued that children's drawing development is largely their developing mastery of particular graphic skills.

It is central to constructivist theories that our perceptual response to an artist's schema has a strong subjective component. Personal memories, our knowledge of artistic style and conventions, our past visual experience all combine to produce the "mental set" which crucially shapes our perceptual response to a picture. According to constructivist theories of perception, therefore, we should expect the development of children's drawings to reflect their invention/acquisition of schemata partly influenced by the artistic culture in which they live (see Wilson and Wilson, 1977). We should also be prepared to find that adults and children respond to children's drawings in quite different ways (see Chapter 9, below).

Among the perceptual theories of pictures, constructivist theories are closest to a symbolic theory of pictures in the role they give to interpretation. Accordingly, like symbolic theory, constructivist theories may be good at accounting for the emotional/expressive aspects of pictures. A constructivist approach may also provide a good account of how our experience with different pictorial styles and devices may mould our subsequent interpretations of pictures or our attempts to make pictures.

Perhaps the major weakness of the constructivist approach as a theory of perception is that it provides no grounds for indicating which of several possible perceptual interpretations of a given set of stimuli are adopted and which are rejected. In principle, there is, in constructivist theory, no restriction on the kinds of perceptual interpretation possible. With regard to pictures, there is no criterion offered by constructivist theory as to which stimuli will be interpreted as a convincing picture by a spectator (see, for example, the critique offered by Hagen, 1980a).

With regard to children's drawings, constructivist theory suggests that children will acquire or invent schemata that suggest perceptual interpretations of their drawings, but the theory does not specify what kinds of factor determine the child's selection of particular schemata. Presumably, there is some intrinsic similarity between the perceptual interpretation stimulated by the picture and the perceptual interpretations the child makes in his/her perceptions of the world, but there are no clear rules to connect the two in constructivist theorizing.

Gestalt theory of picture perception

Gestalt theory of perception is rooted in the work of Wertheimer, Koffka and Kohler (see, for example, Kohler, 1929). A more recent account and critique of Gestalt theory of perception has been provided by Hochberg (1978). Like the constructivist approach, Gestalt psychology considers visual perception to consist of the interpretation of visual input by the viewer. Whereas the constructivist approach stresses the role of experience and culture in our interpretations of sensations, Gestalt psychology proposes that visual input is organized into configurations (*Gestalten*) by fundamental laws of perceptual organization. Gestalt psychologists have claimed that it is impossible to reduce perception to a set of component sensations, as in constructivist theory: in Gestalt terms, perception consists of the organization of stimuli into configurations which are more than (or different from) the sum of their parts.

These Gestalt laws of perceptual organization were believed to be innate and based on physiological mechanisms in the brain. Any given perceptual experience was considered to be the result of the interaction of these physiological mechanisms, brought into play by, and acting upon, the visual stimuli reaching the perceiver. There are echoes of this conception in the work of the late David Marr (1982), whose computational approach to vision stressed the crucial role of the mechanisms involved in detecting visual information and the processing involved in generating a representation of it. Historically, however, the major emphasis of the Gestalt approach was the discovery and study of laws of perceptual organization.

There are many examples of these Gestalt laws of organization; contiguity, closure and common destiny are but three examples. Perhaps one of the most intriguing examples is the principle of figure and ground: given a figural contour, as in Figure 9.b, part of the shape is seen as a figure and the rest is seen as its background. In Figure 9.b there are two alternative and exclusive organizations possible – either a vase or two facial profiles.

Arnheim (1956, 1967, 1969) has been the most influential writer to extend to art the concepts of Gestalt theory of visual perception. Arnheim proposed that the operation of the Gestalt laws of organization enables a perceiver to apprehend the significant structural features or patterns in their visual world. These structures and patterns form what Arnheim calls visual concepts of objects. According to Arnheim (1956), a visual concept of an object has three important properties: it is three-dimensional, of constant shape and not limited to any projective aspect. In addition to the laws of perceptual organization which determine our abstraction of the visual concept of an object, Arnheim (1969) notes that there are three perceptual attitudes which may influence the properties of the visual concept we abstract.

First, there is the everyday perceptual attitude in which we see the object only as an independent entity and we are not aware of the particular perspective view we may have of it at any one moment. In this attitude we are also unaware of the way in which changes in context, such as background and lighting conditions, may affect the momentary appearance of the object. Children's art, according to Arnheim, often exemplifies this everyday perceptual attitude.

Secondly, there is the perceptual attitude in which our visual concept unites the object with its context. As an example, the perceptual ideals of the Impressionist Movement fall into this category of attitude. The Impressionists sought the "real appearance" of an object as determined both by its own nature and by its momentary context (e.g. lighting, background, juxtaposition with other objects). Note that it takes an active effort, and possibly some practice, to see objects in this way. If this "reductive" attitude is achieved, then a given object will change its appearance as the context changes (Arnheim, 1969).

Finally, there is what Arnheim termed the "aesthetic" attitude which produces the most sophisticated kind of visual concept of an object (see Chapter 9). In this attitude the visual concept does not suppress the different aspects of an object but keeps them all present in all-embracing comprehension (Arnheim, 1969). Arnheim gives the example of a cube:

A richer perception observes and enjoys the enchanting and enlightening variety of projectively changing shape. The visual concept of the cube embraces the multiplicity of its appearances, the foreshortenings, the slants, the symmetries and asymmetries, the partial concealments and the deployments, the head-on flatness and the pronounced volumes. (Arnheim, 1969, p. 51)

For Arnheim, a picture is a pattern of marks that stimulates the perception of a visual concept by means of the Gestalt laws of organization. An important feature of Arnheim's theory of pictures is the idea that simple forms may stand for a variety of different objects. He stresses the notion of "structural equivalents" by which he means the graphic symbols that the artist discovers/invents and which stand for an object or part of an object. Any given graphic symbol may be adapted for a variety of different purposes. Thus, in a child's drawing, circles may be used to represent a head, eyes and even the teeth of a saw, all in the same figure (see Arnheim, 1956). (Note that there are some similarities here with Gombrich's notion of a schema and Gibson's conception of pictorial invariants of structure.)

In Arnheim's theory, the production and perception of drawings are closely linked to natural perception of the real world. Both natural perception and picture perception are concerned primarily with overall structure and form, and only secondarily with the differentiation of details. Arnheim then argues that the same priorities apply to children's drawing – early drawings are concerned with the general form of things and become increasingly more differentiated and detailed as the child/artist grows older. Thus, in terms of his Gestalt theory of perception, Arnheim proposes that children do in fact "draw what they see".

Arnheim provides a useful framework within which to discuss the internal structure of pictures in terms of balance, contrast, symmetry, tension and so forth. What Gestalt theory fails to do is provide an account of the conventional element in the interpretation of pictures or provide a systematic integration of stylistic variations in different artistic and cultural traditions (see, for example, the critique offered by Hagen, 1980a).

There are also serious objections to Gestalt theory as an account of perception (see Hochberg, 1978). As regards picture perception, perhaps the main weakness of Gestalt theory is its claim that the whole organization of any perceptual field determines the perception of its component parts. That this assertion is incorrect is suggested by pictures of impossible objects (see Figure 9.a) in which logically incompatible elements within a drawing are combined perceptually to give an impression of a picture of a three-dimensional object.

Summary

It will be clear by now that each theoretical approach provides a useful account of some features of pictures but fails to explain other features equally well. To some extent a hybrid theory seems to offer a compromise: Hagen's generative theory is one such attempt (for further details, see Hagen, 1980b). For present purposes it may be useful to note a similarity between the notion of a schema (from constructivist theory), a pictorial invariant of structure (from Gibson's ecological theory) and Arnheim's suggestion of a visual concept. The important common core to all these conceptions is the idea that a set of marks on a flat surface may elicit a perceptual response that is related to, but not identical with, perception of the real world.

The differences between these conceptions seem to us also to be important because each identifies a distinct and important element in picture making and picture perceiving: constructivist theories stress the ways in which pictures have to be constructed using graphic devices to achieve pictorial effects. They also provide a role for experience and convention in shaping perceptual interpretations of simplified (and often ambiguous) pictorial stimuli. Ecological "invariant" theory points out the extent to which natural perception and pictures are often concerned with the general appearance and structure of objects and scenes (common in much child art). Gestalt theory provides an analysis that suggests that our response to certain forms and patterns may be innately determined by the operation of the Gestalt laws of perceptual organization.

To summarize, then: a child's drawing is a commonplace of everyday life and yet it introduces conceptual complexities such that experts cannot agree on exactly what a drawing is. It is usually a representation of something, although we must allow for the possibility of non-representational scribbles and patterns. As a representation we may try to understand it both as something related to natural perception, but also as a symbol which is interpreted as part of a symbol system.

4 Why do children draw?

Having considered the difficulties of defining what a picture is, we can now turn to the conceptually easier matter of why children draw. Here we can conveniently start with an observation of our own – that pre-school children may make many drawings at a sitting but show not the slightest interest in any of them once they are completed, let alone show them to anyone else. It is nearly always parents and teachers, not the children, who put drawings on display. It seems to us, and to others, that drawing is often a relatively solitary activity. In consequence, most theories of children's drawing have assumed, implicitly or explicitly, that children make drawings largely for the satisfaction they get from the activity itself. As we shall see, few theorists have given detailed consideration to reasons for drawing and relevant research is scarce. For our discussion, we have adopted the grouping of theories and approaches first presented in Chapter 1.

Developmental approaches

Drawing as play
A useful way to begin our consideration of why children draw is to think of drawing as a kind of play behaviour. We can then examine the motives and functions which different developmental approaches have assigned to play in general and to drawing in particular. Children themselves certainly seem to regard drawing as a form of play, engaging in it willingly and becoming absorbed in it much as they do in their solitary play with toys and materials. Many different theories have been proposed to account for play and we next consider some of these theories and evaluate their usefulness in understanding why children draw.

One of the earliest theories of play is that human beings are innately disposed to be active, and that play is a way of discharging surplus energy (Schiller, 1875). This theory does not provide a very plausible explanation for drawing, which typically requires only modest expenditure of energy. Furthermore, Levy (1978) notes that, as a general explanation of play, the surplus energy theory fails both to distinguish between different forms of play and to account for the absence of play in certain populations of children, such as the mentally handicapped living in institutions (see Phemister, Richardson and Thomas, 1978).

The pre-exercise theory of play (Groos, 1901) also appeals to an instinct for play; and, like the surplus energy theory, cannot explain why certain populations of (deprived) children show so little spontaneous play (see Smilansky, 1968). Furthermore, the emphasis placed on instinctive tendencies by Groos assigns only a secondary role to (likely important) environmental and cultural factors and gives no indication of how such factors might operate. The pre-exercise theory, however, did introduce the important idea that play provides the child with an important opportunity to practise and perfect activities and skills necessary in subsequent adult life (Levy, 1978; see also Bruner, 1972). Applied to drawing, the pre-exercise theory suggests that in their artwork children are practising and developing skills that will be important to them when they grow up.

Are there any adult activities for which children's drawing might conceivably constitute relevant preparation? Van Sommers (1984) identifies several kinds of adult drawing activity. Among varieties of public drawing he notes the drawing of maps, plans and organizational trees to communicate and explain. Engineers' and designers' drawings can communicate and also function as an aid to thinking and planning. Van Sommers also identifies some private drawing activities, some of which seem essentially similar in function to public drawing for planning and designing. Drawings of room plans, dress designs and flow-charts all fall into this category. Other kinds of private drawing identified by van Sommers seem to be more recreational in nature and are thus closer to children's drawing. Examples of such recreational drawing identified by van

Sommers in a survey of everyday graphic output included doodling and drawings made to express feelings.

It seems not unreasonable to assume that children's drawing activities provide a helpful foundation for the later development of adult graphic skill. Related to this is Arnheim's idea that much thinking is basically perceptual in character, with the implication that early drawing practice could play an important part in visual training in all fields of learning. Arnheim (1969) has argued forcefully that visual training is much neglected in contemporary education. Furthermore, it may be that the practice of using a system of pictorial symbols in drawing facilitates the child's subsequent acquisition and use of other representational systems such as mathematics and written language. In support of this notion, work on literacy development has suggested pictorial origins for some aspects of children's early writing (Ferreiro, 1985). That said, there is as yet no systematically collected evidence either to confirm or contradict these hypotheses.

Yet another early biological theory of play, the recapitulation theory (Hall, 1906), suggested that play consists of the rehearsal of instinctive activities important to our ancestors. The value of play, according to Hall, is that it provides an outlet for the discharge of primitive instincts (e.g. aggression) that might otherwise prove troublesome in contemporary society. While drawing itself is not likely to be a rehearsal of instinctive activities, it might allow the discharge of primitive instincts in a symbolic form. A small boy, for example, who draws pictures of soldiers and battles could (arguably) be said to be rehearsing and discharging primitive aggressive impulses. This interesting notion reappears in a different guise in psychoanalytic theories of play and drawing (see below). As with the other biological theories, however, recapitulation theory can be criticized for its neglect of environmental and cultural influences.

Piaget's account of drawing

Piaget's account of intellectual development still dominates developmental approaches to children's drawing (Piaget and Inhelder, 1969). Piaget did not propose a theory of drawing as such; he used drawing as a source of evidence for his theory of the child's developing representation of the world. Drawing, for Piaget, was halfway between symbolic play and mental images. An understanding of this position, however, requires us to take a closer look at Piaget's general theory of intellectual development and of the function of play.

According to Piaget, the growth of intelligence in childhood progresses through a series of stages at a rate that is largely determined by biological maturation and, therefore, the age of the child. As a consequence, in Piaget's system learning from experience plays a somewhat limited role in cognitive development.

Piaget proposed that interactions with the environment take the form of either assimilation or accommodation. In assimilation, the developing child tries to make sense of the environment by using existing cognitive structures and ideas. If a new experience cannot be assimilated using existing cognitive structures, then those structures are adapted through the process of accommodation. Accommodation, therefore, involves adjusting to new features of the environment and to new information.

In the natural way of things, the young child is constantly faced with the necessity of accommodating (adapting) to an external social and physical world which is largely beyond his/her control and which s/he understands only slightly. It is therefore necessary for the child's emotional and mental equilibrium, according to Piaget, for there to be an area of activity that is not so externally constrained and that provides opportunities for assimilation. Play is the main activity involving assimilation. In symbolic play, for example, children are able to re-live events and important experiences and so come to make sense of them. The pleasure of play is that experiences thus re-lived can be modified to suit the whim and wishes of the player:

If there is a scene at lunch, for example, one can be sure that an hour or two afterward it will be re-created with dolls and will be brought to a happier solution. Either the child disciplines her doll more intelligently than her parents did her, or in play she accepts what she had not accepted at lunch (such as finishing a bowl of soup she does not like, especially if here it is the doll who finishes it symbolically). (Piaget and Inhelder, 1969, p.60)

Some of children's drawing, according to Piaget, shares with play the quality of being done for its own sake and providing opportunities for assimilation. Thus, for example, Piaget regards the early scribbles of very young children as being "pure play". We can also note that the rationale for using art as therapy is similar to Piaget's concept of assimilation. To the extent that children use their drawing to recreate personally important incidents, then that drawing could serve an assimilative function. It is not at all clear, however, whether children do in fact frequently produce drawings for this purpose (see Chapter 5).

Unlike other forms of play, however, Piaget regarded most drawing as also an attempt to represent the real world, which therefore had much in common with the emergence of mental images. Indeed, he seems to have been interested in children's drawing principally as a source of evidence to support his theories of the child's developing representation of the real world and especially the conception of space (see Selfe, 1983). Piaget's view that cognitive development proceeds through a series of discrete stages led him to adopt with enthusiasm the classification of stages in children's drawing development originally proposed by Luquet (1913). The drawings typical of each of these stages Piaget took to be an accurate reflection of the child's developing conception of spatial geometry (see Chapters 1, 2 and 6).

It is not explicit in Piaget's writing, however, exactly why children should wish to make graphic representations of mental images (see below). A further objection to the Piagetian view of intellectual development is that the discrete demarcation of development into stages is misleading, especially with regard to the development of drawing. Cross-cultural comparisons (see Deregowski, 1980; Alland, 1983) have challenged the notion of universal stages of drawing development, and experimental psychologists (see Freeman, 1980) have objected that the emphasis on biologically derived developmental stages obscures the important contribution of planning strategies and other task features of the drawing process.

Clinical-projective approaches

The dominant theory underlying clinical-projective approaches to children's drawing is psychoanalytic theory. It would be hard to underestimate the influence of this theory on current and recent thinking about play in general and drawing in particular. Psychoanalytic theory originated in the clinical work of Sigmund Freud, but there have been many subsequent revisions and variations. Central to later versions of the theory is the concept of the unconscious mind as the source of complementary drives for (erotic sexual) gratification and for aggression/destruction. Freud suggested that these instinctive drives engendered wishes and impulses that were often threatening or unacceptable and so were kept from conscious awareness. Although not directly accessible to consciousness, such wishes could, according to psychoanalytic theory, nevertheless influence behaviour or manifest themselves in some other form or disguise (Freud, 1976).

With regard to drawing, Freud's theories indicate that a child's artwork will be strongly influenced by his/her unconscious wishes and fears, although expression of these wishes may be in a symbolic or disguised form. To take a typical example, Hammer cited the case of a teenage girl who, "heavily oppressed by the frictions and constant heated arguments at home, mirrored this in her drawing of the House by adding a profusion of thick, bellowing smoke pouring forth from the chimney. In this matter, the drawing reflected her view of her home as a hot-bed of turbulence, unrest and stirred-up emotionality" (1958, p. 167). The presumption of such projection of emotions forms the rationale for the widespread use of children's drawings as tests for emotional adjustment. We should note, however, that adequately controlled investigations have generally failed to find support for projective interpretations (see Chapter 7).

In terms of motivation for drawing, an important aspect of psychoanalytic theory is the idea that the expression of unconscious wishes and feelings, even in disguised form in a drawing, serves as a "safety valve" which provides a harmless discharge for feelings which would otherwise be "bottled up" and possibly dangerous. This psychoanalytic idea, that drawing may allow the catharsis (purging) of repressed emotions, bears a resemblance to recapitulation theory, which suggests that play provides an opportunity for the harmless expression of instinctive impulses (see above). This idea forms part of the rationale for art therapy (see Chapter 7).

Later developments of psychoanalytic theory have introduced two further factors as possible reasons for drawing and play: the need to be grown up and the need to assume an active role and to be in control. Thus, for example, Erikson (1968, p. 351) wrote that play "often proves to be the infantile way of thinking over difficult experiences and of restoring a sense of mastery". Applying this argument to children's art suggests that children may find drawing satisfying if it provides them with a sense of mastery over the medium as well as the topics and situations portrayed.

Consistent with this notion, once a child has mastered a schema for a drawing topic, s/he may use it again and again, becoming more and more observant and interested in portraying it as realistically as possible and adjusting the design and/or shape (see, for example, Goodnow, 1977). It is also common to find that children will develop a theme in their drawing and make drawings of the same topic over and over again. One six-year-old boy we know at one time repeatedly drew battlefield scenes depicting soldiers of various kinds in a variety of combat situations. He was not necessarily expressing personal experiences or feelings of violence, and the images may simply have been copied from comic-strips and television (Wilson and Wilson, 1977). That said, it may also have been very satisfying to exert control over such scenes; and, of course, there is likely to be gender-linked pressure for boys to show interest in battles rather than, say, flowers.

Artistic approaches

Sensory/perceptual factors

Many authors have suggested that the sensory feedback from drawing can be satisfying, especially for very young children taking their first steps in drawing. Kellogg (1970) has distinguished between "motor pleasure" and "visual pleasure" that children can gain from drawing. Motor pleasure is presumed to be derived from the movements that the child makes in scribbling; visual pleasure comes from inspecting the product of the drawing or scribbling. Kellogg (1970) has argued that the visual component must be dominant, if not essential, because children quickly stop scribbling with a crayon or pen that fails to leave a mark (see also Gardner, 1980).

To say that the production of marks is satisfying is in itself not a very useful explanation. Of more interest are the suggestions of several authors who have hypothesized that certain configurations and patterns of marks will be perceptually satisfying. Arnheim (1956), for example, proposed that visual balance in a drawing will be naturally and universally satisfying. Arnheim has produced many interesting and convincing analyses of both child and adult art in these terms. The notion of visual balance is, we think, implicit in judgements of the composition of a picture. The elements in what we call a well-composed picture are usually in balance so that each side of the picture has equivalent visual weight. Indeed, Arnheim seems to regard some aesthetic principles, such as "good form", as innate – a view that is still popular. The idea of innate aesthetic principles is, of course, consistent with Arnheim's Gestalt theory that all perception is produced and shaped by innate principles of organization, such as the grouping of similar elements and closure. Another related principle is that of symmetry. Children have been found to be especially sensitive to, and have preferences for, patterns displaying bilateral symmetry (see Chapter 9).

Rhoda Kellogg (1970) is another well-known author who has claimed that children's drawing is constructed out of basic forms that are intrinsically attractive. The evidence she cites for this claim is that simple forms, such as circles, rectangles, crosses and mandalas (a circle containing a cross), can be found in the drawings of children of many different ages and cultural backgrounds. Further evidence cited by Kellogg, that there is a "primary visual order" which is innate and universal, is that the very same forms frequently recur in the abstract and early pictorial motifs of prehistoric and indigenous art all over the world.

A problem here is that Kellogg's analyses were not systematic, and we do not know how representative many of her examples are of the art of children or of primitive cultures. Furthermore, as Freeman (1980) has noted, a problem with many of these ideas of universals of good form is that we have yet to establish whether children do in fact use these suggested criteria in the production and evaluation of their drawings. It is possible, for example, that children frequently use circles in their drawing, not because the circle is intrinsically attractive to them, but because it is a pictorially useful, general-purpose shape which is easy for them to make. Furthermore, other researchers who have studied drawing in different cultures (see Alland, 1983, for example) have been doubtful that the occurrence and appeal of basic pictorial shapes such as the mandala is as universal as Kellogg has claimed. These questions require more scientific research than they have so far received.

Representational purpose

Many authorities have implicitly or explicitly assumed that a major reason why children make drawings is to make graphic representations; that is to say, pictures. Freeman (1980), for example, has implied that picture making is the main reason for drawing, but, like many others, has not elaborated further as to why picture making should be so rewarding.

Arnheim (1956) noted that children aim to draw symbols and implied that artistic expression in pictorial symbols is universally satisfying. Kellogg (1970) also suggested that children's art has a symbolizing purpose. Selfe (1983) presumably intended a similar claim when she noted that the purpose of drawing is to produce a satisfying symbol of aspects of visual and emotional experience. In a similar vein, Gardner (1980) has suggested that an important reason for drawing is the expression of "feelings". Lowenfeld has long claimed that self-expression (of feelings and emotions) in art provides great satisfaction and, therefore, is a major reason for drawing (see Lowenfeld and Brittain, 1975).

It is clear, then, that many authorities agree that children draw because they find it satisfying to produce pictures – in particular, pictures that symbolize and express their interests and experiences. This notion is certainly consistent with children's choices of drawing topic. In most studies of children's representational drawings, the human figure has been found to be the most popular topic (e.g. Maitland, 1895; Lukens, 1896; Ballard, 1912; Luquet, 1913). Houses and animals have also been found to be popular topics. More recently, Koppitz (1968) and Lark-Horovitz, Lewis and Luca (1967) have concluded that animals, houses, cars, boats, planes and flowers are all popular topics of children's drawings, but that children most often draw human figures.

Much research has indicated that there are some sex differences in choice of drawing topic. Studies using the "draw-a-person" test have repeatedly shown that children have a preference for drawing figures of their own sex (Machover, 1949; Koppitz, 1968; Papadakis, 1989). This preference for drawing own-sex figures is interpreted as a consequence of the child identifying with his/her own sex. Other sex differences have been reported by Levy and Levy (1958), who found, after collecting some 2,000 drawings of animals by adolescents, that more boys drew snakes, fish and horses and that more girls drew cats, rabbits and dogs.

There are some predictable cultural influences on choice of subject matter. Anastasi and Foley (1936) concluded that the general choice of drawing topic was more or less the same in the forty-two countries they studied. However, certain animals were favoured in certain countries (such as the camel in Africa and the cow in India), as were certain occupations when depicted in human figure drawings. Anastasi and Foley, therefore, came to the unsurprising conclusion that religion, traditions, economic situations and so forth all play an important role in the choice of subject matter by the six- to twelve-year-old children they studied (see also Lark-Horovitz, Lewis and Luca, 1967).

One special form of cultural influence on the subject matter of children's drawings is the child's experience of other people's drawings and pictures. Such material is often copied by children and thus may powerfully influence the topics and character of their drawing. Wilson and Wilson (1977) interviewed 147 college and high school students about their drawings. In every case the image drawn by the student could be traced back to some previously existing graphic source that the student had copied or adapted. They also found that children from a milieu rich in models, pictures, books and so forth would produce more drawing schemata, which were better developed, compared to the drawings of a child from an environment lacking such models.

There is, however, little direct evidence available to support the claim that children find picture making rewarding other than the observation that they do frequently make a lot of pictures. It can, admittedly, sometimes be useful to identify rewarding activities by observing how frequently they occur (cf. Premack, 1959). For an adequate theory of motivation for drawing, however, we need something more than the circular reasoning that because children make a lot of pictures then they must find picture making satisfying, which is why they make a lot of pictures. Part of the problem is that theories of self-expression and representation in drawing have not been very precisely formulated. It has not been made clear, for example, what the consequences would be if children were denied appropriate means of self-expression in art. It would be of interest to know whether children denied outlets for representational activity in drawing would seek other outlets for symbolic expression, such as pretend play and story-telling.

We must not forget, however, that not all of children's art is representational or symbolic. Alland (1983) compared art from pre-school children in six different countries, and found that in a culture without a strong tradition of visual art, children drew formally organized pictures, but without any obvious representational or symbolic meaning.

Social influences

Although it seems likely that the primary motivation for drawing is intrinsic to the activity itself, we should not ignore several potentially important external social influences on drawing. Fairly obviously, adults can influence the amount of drawing undertaken by a child to the extent to which they make drawing materials available. Some parents may actively encourage drawing by showing children how to make simple drawings and telling stories about them. It is undoubtedly true that most children enjoy being praised for their drawings: children will sometimes take their pictures to be admired. In other families, however, drawing may be ignored or even actively discouraged; for example, because of religious traditions which proscribe the production (and worship) of images. Older children and adolescents are widely believed to make fewer drawings than do younger children, perhaps, as Kellogg (1970) has claimed, because adults, including school teachers, may actively disparage drawing by older children as an immature and childish activity.

Many children's drawings, in particular those made by older children, can readily and immediately be understood by others. Consequently, it is reasonable to consider at least some of children's drawings as attempts to communicate and, therefore, that communicating with others is sometimes part of children's motivation to make drawings.

Summary

It is apparent that it is not easy to give a totally convincing answer to the question of why children draw. It seems reasonable to suppose that different children at different times have different reasons for drawing. Sometimes young children may simply relish the creation of marks on paper or the production of aesthetically satisfying shapes. Other, perhaps older, children may derive satisfaction from the creation of recognizable pictures of topics which interest them. For some the pleasure of drawing may be the creation of a symbolic world in which they can exercise the control which they lack in real life. Related to this last reason is the idea that drawing serves an expressive purpose and that the expression of emotional experience is both deeply satisfying and necessary for emotional health. While all these proposed motivations seem plausible, it is rare to find independent evidence for their validity.

5 The drawing process and its effects

Now that we know something of what pictures are and why children draw them, we can begin to consider the process of actually constructing a drawing. As we have already indicated, a great deal of investigation of children's drawing has considered only the finished pictures that children draw. This preoccupation with what Freeman has called the "surface structure" of drawings united both the intelligence and personality assessment traditions of the analysis of drawings. Furthermore, as noted in Chapter 1, Piaget's developmental account of drawing was also limited to surface structure. Recently, however, several investigators (e.g. Olsen, 1970; Freeman, 1972, 1980; Goodnow, 1977) have argued convincingly that the effects of the drawing process cannot be ignored. On the contrary, the processes children use to construct drawings are at least as important as any supposed underlying mental image in determining the form of the finished drawing. As we shall see, the process of constructing a drawing is much more complex than a simple translation of a mental image onto paper.

A study by Phillips, Inall and Lauder (1985) provides an interesting demonstration of the complexities of the drawing process and some indication of the requirements for making an adequate graphic representation. Phillips *et al.* asked six- and seven-year-old children to draw pictures of a cube and of a pyramid, which they viewed through a reduction tube giving an oblique view of the object. Of course, it is unlikely that any of the children had ever spontaneously drawn a cube or pyramid before, let alone in a way that conveyed depth information (see Chapter 6). As was to be expected, very few of the children drew anything like an oblique projection of the object viewed. The children were then given training in which they watched the experimenter draw an oblique projection of one of the objects, one step at a time. In a subsequent retest they then made very much closer approximations to an oblique projection in their own drawing. However, a similar amount of visual training on the properties of a cube or a pyramid had no significant effect, and training on just one object produced no improvement on drawings of the other. Phillips *et al.* concluded that successful drawing of any object requires more than just a good knowledge of the visual properties of that object. They argued that in order to make a representational drawing of an object a child must first acquire an adequate "graphic description" of that object. A graphic description of an object may be quite different from its functional description. Thus, for example, the functional properties of a cube (square sides, stable, stackable and so forth) do not translate obviously into the graphic properties of an oblique projection of a cube on paper.

The concept of a graphic description is not new. In the context of adult art the notion of a schema, and its crucial importance in picture making generally, has been extensively discussed by Gombrich (1972). Gombrich's important and influential analysis has led him to conclude that without schemata (graphic descriptions) and knowledge of a variety of pictorial devices no picture making would be possible. (See our discussion of constructivist theory in Chapter 3.) An important part of the history of art, indeed, is the discovery and development of schemata for depicting different objects and scenes. To some extent we can also see that in learning to draw, the task facing a child is one of acquiring a graphic description for each of a variety of topics (see discussion of schemata below).

The recognition that making a drawing is a complex activity means that any rational interpretation of drawings for what they might reveal about the drawer's emotional and intellectual condition must take into account the processes involved in constructing those drawings. As Freeman (1972) pointed out, some of the more striking features of young children's drawing may be by-products of drawing strategies rather than reflections of children's conceptions of the topic portrayed. Quite obviously, the strategies used by children in making drawings are of interest in their own right because of what they reveal about the development of representational schemata and of planning and organizing skills. In addition, an understanding of the effects of those strategies is also an essential requirement for any adequate interpretation of a drawing for its emotional or conceptual content (see Chapters 6 and 7).

Compositional styles

A good place to start our discussion is with the observation that young children typically construct their pictures from a limited "vocabulary" of simple shapes and lines (see Fenson, 1985). In contrast, drawings of older children often contain continuous contours in which a complex shape is produced with an embracing outline. Goodnow (1977) has used the term "threading" to describe outline drawing in this way, because the production of such a contour is a little like laying out a thread. Some typical constructed and threaded outline drawings are shown in Figures 10.a and 10.b.

These two compositional styles – constructing and outlining – are not mutually exclusive. Outline drawings with complex contours may still be partly constructed, as when a few simple shapes are added to a complex contour (see Figure 10.c). As Fenson (1985) has noted, constructed drawings have a distinctive child-like appearance, and over the age range of four to eight years it appears that constructed drawings gradually give way to outline drawings for many children (see also Goodnow, 1977). Fenson points to two advantages of outlining. First, more realistic drawings are possible – the constructional style artificially segments figures into simple component shapes which are not apparent in the real world. Outlining avoids this problem. Second, outlining makes it possible to draw figures in a variety of different orientations (e.g. in profile, full face and in oblique projection) and engaged in a variety of activities (running, jumping and so forth) which would be harder to portray in a drawing constructed of component shapes. Although drawing in these two styles differs in some important ways, there are many design and performance problems common to both. It is these problems to which we now turn.

Graphic vocabulary

Simple shapes

Many authors (e.g. Arnheim, 1956; Kellogg, 1970; Goodnow, 1977; Freeman, 1980; Willats, 1981, 1985) have noted that children's constructed drawings are typically composed of a relatively few shapes and lines. The construction of many varied pictures from a few simple shapes is possible because, as many investigators have noted, one shape can represent very many different things. Consider Figure 7.a, which presents a four-year-old's drawing of a man and a dog. In this picture, lines serve as:

1. contours indicating the outline of the dog's body,
2. the collapsed contours of the lead and the man's arm, and
3. cracks indicating the mouth of both man and dog.

The drawing also makes (typically) extensive use of the circle, one of the first enclosed forms made by most children (Arnheim, 1956). In Figure 7.b circles (arguably) represent solid objects – the head of the man and the dog. Other circles represent plane surfaces – the discs of the eyes. Further possible uses for circles in drawing include the representation of hoops and holes.

Arnheim, in particular, considers that the circle is of special importance in children's drawing development. He called it the "primordial circle". According to him, "The circle is the simplest possible shape available in the pictorial medium. Until shape becomes differentiated, the circle does not stand for roundness, but for any shape at all and none in particular" (Arnheim, 1956, p. 140). Arnheim believed that perceptual organization develops from simple forms into more complex ones. Thus, children only gradually come to differentiate the particular shapes of objects and surfaces, both in perception and in their drawing. According to this argument, very young children do not attempt to indicate the precise shape of the things they portray in their drawing. They use simple forms to represent objects, regardless of whether or not the precise shape of the form matches that of the object portrayed.

Figure 11.a shows a drawing of a house, a man and a dog made by a four-year-old girl. Note how the circle is used for the head (and possibly also the body) of the man and dog, and also for the house itself. Similarly with respect to surfaces, circles are used to indicate eyes on the figures and windows on the house. While taking no stand on Arnheim's claim that circles have cosmic appeal, we can readily agree with his conclusion that circles are almost universal in children's drawing and in many cases become the first pictures that a child will make.

Freeman (1980) reports an investigation in which he presented children (aged between eight and twelve years) with pre-drawn circles which they were asked to "turn into as many different sorts of drawing as possible". Freeman reported a strong bias towards considering a circle as the contour of a solid object (rather than as a hole or a plane surface). We also know that experience of pictures is not necessary for the recognition of objects portrayed in line drawings (see Hochberg and Brooks, 1962). Hochberg and Brooks found that a child raised without opportunities to associate pictures with objects or their names could still correctly identify line drawings of objects such as a shoe, a doll and a motor car (see also Chapter 3).

These findings are consistent with arguments first put forward by perceptual psychologists (e.g. Rubin, 1915) that there is a tendency to perceive a line as the contour of a solid object and thus as dividing the picture's surface into figure and background. We need take no stand here on whether or not perception of figure and ground in a line drawing is necessary for shape perception, nor whether such discriminations are innate or learned from our everyday experience of the world. We know, however, that a line is not inevitably seen as the contour of an object - see, for example, the lines indicating the mouth of the man and the dog in Figure 7.a.

It is difficult to say whether or not very young children discover the pictorial potential of these primitive shapes and lines for themselves in the course of scribbling, or whether they learn from parents, peers and picture books. Some graphic conventions are almost certainly learned from others, such as a flattened "m" for a flying bird, but other devices may well be discoveries/inventions that children often make for themselves. Research by Wilson and Wilson (1977) suggests that older children acquire a great many graphic devices by copying from previously existing material (see our discussion of schemata below).

Pattern and movement preferences

The drawing of a shape, whether simple or complex, involves a number of decisions. Drawing a circle probably presents the fewest problems (see Arnheim, 1956): the three main decisions are where to start, which direction to take (clockwise or anticlockwise) and how big. Goodnow (1977) has provided quite a detailed review and discussion of the biases children bring to these decisions. She reported that much early research on these pattern and production preferences was carried out by Ilg and Ames (1965), two associates of Gesell, who were primarily interested in determining developmental sequences to decide when children were ready for formal schooling. This, and subsequent research by Goodnow and Levine (1973) on the copying of simple patterns, has indicated that a number of fairly general principles apply to the production of shapes. There is, for example, a common tendency to start drawing near the top of the paper and to move from left to right. Many American children start drawing circles in a clockwise fashion, but switch to the anti-clockwise direction often taught for writing. While many sequential preferences of this kind undoubtedly reflect the influence of writing, Goodnow concluded that some other factors must also be involved. A preference for starting at the top and at the left, for example, seems to appear at an age before children learn to read or write, and to persist regardless of the usual direction of the script they learn to use (English, Arabic, Hebrew and so forth).

These sequential preferences can account for a number of features of children's drawing. Goodnow (1977) has reported that schoolchildren usually draw trains moving to the left. The reason for this preference, she argued, is that the direction of movement is governed by the positioning of the engine, which is normally drawn first on the left-hand side of the page.

A preference for starting at the top may also explain why the majority of children (at least in Western countries) start their drawings of people with the head (see, for example, Freeman, 1980; Thomas and Tsalimi, 1988). The decision to draw the head first then has further consequences for the proportions of the rest of the drawing (see our discussion of sequencing below). Freeman (1980) has also argued that an end-anchoring effect may explain why three- and four-year-old children are more likely to draw the head and legs than the arms and trunk in their drawing of a human figure. The head and legs define the upper and lower extremities of the dominant vertical axis of the figure.

Several authors, but most notably Arnheim (1956) and Kellogg (1970), have appealed to children's aesthetic preferences to explain features of their drawing. Thus, for example, Arnheim claimed that children have a preference for patterns and pictures that are balanced visually. Kellogg proposed that symmetry, particularly radial symmetry, has a universal appeal which, she claimed, accounted for the popularity of the mandala pattern in children's drawing and in primitive art (see Figure 3.b; Chapter 2).

As Freeman (1980) has pointed out, one problem with these proposals is that there have been very few attempts independently to assess children's preferences for particular patterns or kinds of symmetry. It is not safe to conclude that children have a preference for symmetry (for example) on the grounds that their drawings are sometimes symmetrical. We need an independent assessment of preference to exclude other possible explanations.

Putting shapes and lines together

Combining simple shapes and lines to make more complex pictures is, as we have noted, one of the hallmarks of young children's drawing. We should not underestimate the difficulties that the construction of such combinations can present. Such constructed drawings have to be planned: first, decisions have to be taken about the order of drawing the component parts; second, when positioning the first-drawn elements, space has to be reserved for parts which will be added later in the drawing sequence; finally, later-drawn elements of the picture have to be positioned so that they can be joined on to previously drawn elements as appropriate. There are now good reasons to think that many quite distinctive features of children's drawing are products of the construction problems of positioning, sequencing and planning.

Positioning

A good place to start our consideration of construction problems is with human figure drawing. The human figure is a universally popular topic of children's free drawing (see Chapter 4) and drawings of the human figure have been more extensively investigated than those of any other topic. For very young children a major problem is the relative positioning of the parts of the body. Figure 4.b presents a drawing of a man made by a three-year-old. The picture looks unrecognizable to most adults, but questioning the child revealed that the scribble is a picture containing representations of teeth, eyes, stomach and legs. The failure to position and connect the elements correctly is typical of early representational drawings and is termed synthetic incapability (see Chapter 2). It is possible that the child who drew the picture may not have even attempted to connect the parts of her drawing. As we shall see later, failures of positioning made by older children are most likely to be the result of misjudgements rather than lack of concern.

Figure 4.b does, however, illustrate very clearly a construction principle that is regarded as one of the hallmarks of children's drawing (Goodnow, 1977). Each of the parts of the body shown in Figure 4.b has been allocated its own space on the paper. None of the parts overlaps another, even in cases (such as ears and hair) where they would do so in a visually correct projection. As we shall see below, this tendency not to overlap the component parts of a drawing becomes an important factor when children start to arrange shapes together to make more complex pictures.

Sequencing

When simple shapes are arranged together in a drawing there are a number of decisions to be made – which shapes to draw first, where to draw them and how to join them together. Children's solutions to these problems can have major consequences for the appearance of the finished drawing.

It has long been noted, for example, that young children

often draw the head relatively too large (see Figure 12). Several hypotheses can be offered to explain this dominance of the head. If we accept the (historically important) view that children's drawings directly reflect their conceptions or mental representations of the topics portrayed, then we should have to conclude that children consider heads to be relatively larger than they really are. Another possibility is that children consider heads to be more important than the rest of the body and so draw them relatively larger to signal that importance. The conventional use of size to signal importance is a feature of some early Egyptian art, for example, but there is no clear evidence that it is a widespread feature of children's drawing (see Arnheim, 1956; and Chapter 7 below).

In contrast, Freeman (1980) has suggested that the dominance of the head has more to do with the sequence in which children draw than with their internal representations of the human figure. Specifically, Freeman proposed that children normally draw the head before the body and that head size overestimation can result if children fail to leave sufficient space for a visually correct depiction of the trunk and the legs.

Thomas and Tsalimi (1988) have confirmed that the majority of children do indeed draw the head before the body, and that the few children who spontaneously draw the trunk or legs first do not show the usual overestimation of the head. In a second experiment, Thomas and Tsalimi persuaded children to abandon their normally preferred order of drawing the head first by asking them to start with the trunk instead. When this was done, the resulting drawings displayed head/body proportions which were close to the visually correct ratio of approximately 1:6, and showed little evidence of the usual relative overestimation of the size of the head. Finally, in examination of the drawings of a control group of children who had been asked to start their drawings with the head (i.e. the usual spontaneously preferred order), it was found that a significant number of the children had not left enough room for a visually correct drawing of the trunk and legs beneath the head.

Given that it is easier to plan and execute a correctly proportioned figure if the part requiring the most space is drawn first, then it is of interest to ask why children normally prefer to draw in an order that is inherently more difficult. One possibility is that there are performance biases, natural or acquired, which lead children to start drawing near the top of the page (see above). Another possibility is that the head is drawn first because it is considered the most important part of the body. To test this latter hypothesis requires us to make an independent enquiry into the importance children assign to the various parts of the body – an enquiry that might not be easy to do in practice.

Planning

Another reason why the head may be drawn too large in relation to the body is that the outline drawn for the head normally contains the facial details, whereas the outline of the body is often left blank. Thus children, perhaps uncertain of their fine motor control, enlarge the outline of the head to make sure that there will be enough space to show the eyes, nose and mouth (see Freeman, 1980). Henderson and Thomas, in an unpublished study, investigated this hypothesis by requesting the depiction of specific details in children's draw-ings of a man (see Figure 13). Asking children to show the man's teeth resulted in heads which were drawn relatively even larger than usual, asking for buttons and pockets to be drawn on the man's jacket increased the size of the trunk relative to that of the head. Finally, asking for a man to be drawn from behind, so that his face could not be seen, reduced the outline of the head relative to that of the trunk. These results indicate that children may plan the size of the outlines drawn for head and trunk in anticipation of the amount of detail they intend to include within the outline. Given this finding, it also seems likely that the common overestimation of the size of the head is at least partly a consequence of the greater amount of detail usually included in the outline of the head compared to the trunk.

Planning for the inclusion of detail may also influence the overall size of figures and not just the relative sizes of parts of a figure. Silk and Thomas (1988) found that children asked to draw a house, a man and a dog could produce correct ordinal size scaling of the figures (house bigger than man, man bigger than dog). However, the size of the dog was overestimated relative to the man, and the size of the man was overestimated relative to the house (see Figure 11). Silk and Thomas argued that the overestimation was not easy to explain in terms of the relative importance of the topics, nor of children's conceptions of them. Instead, they proposed that the children were essentially aiming at a visually correct depiction of the sizes of the figures, but that they differentially increased the size of the smaller figures (man and dog) to ensure that there would be enough space within the outlines for the inclusion of details. In contrast, the outline of the house, being very much larger, provided enough space for the portrayal of all the anticipated detail without exaggerating its size.

The tendency for children to give each part of a drawing its own space on the paper (see above) continues even when they progress to connecting the various parts together. Problems caused by competition for space are likely to be most severe where the drawer has not planned ahead in starting to draw and consequently not left an appropriate space for the parts to be drawn later. Goodnow (1977) argues that some of the very "queer" looking drawings which children produce are a consequence of their efforts not to overlap parts for which they have not left adequate space. In the drawing of a girl in Figure 14, for example, the hair (drawn early in the proceedings) cuts across the space where you would normally expect the arms to go. Faced with the subsequent problem of drawing the arms, Goodnow (1977) reports that the solution of actually drawing the arms across the hair is relatively rare in children's spontaneous free drawing.

There are, however, several solutions which children commonly adopt to avoid overlapping parts such as arms and hair. First, the arms could be relocated wherever there is space available rather than in their proper place. Thus, for example, many children would draw the arms further down the figure, so that they seemed to be attached at the knees. A second and commonly preferred solution would be to leave out the arms altogether. Another possible solution would be to draw the arms so that they point downwards at a steep angle.

Another consequence of the planning problems encountered in making a drawing is that young children may be more inclined to draw features (such as hats) which are not likely to be in competition with many other parts of the body for available space (see Goodnow, 1977). In contrast, we have observed that features such as spectacles (which must be at least as common as hats in children's everyday experiences) are drawn much less frequently, presumably in part because there is often no space to include them without overlapping other parts of the drawing.

Schemata

We have argued above that a successful picture is always based on a graphic description of how to put lines together to generate a representation of the topic in question. The term schema is often applied to such a graphic description when the drawer produces the same combination of forms or patterns repeatedly (often to represent different topics) and constructs many pictures using the same formula. The repeated use of a particular form and sequence in drawing is especially apparent in the drawings of children aged from three to six years of age, hence the term "schematic" has been used to describe this period of drawing development. An example of the use of a schema is illustrated in Figure 11.a, in which the same basic figure plan has been used to produce drawings of a house, a man and a dog. While many authorities have remarked on children's use of schemata (see, for example, Barnhart, 1942; Goodnow, 1977; Freeman, 1980; Gardner, 1980), there has been relatively little systematic investigation of the use of schemata and their effects on children's drawing.

Most authors agree, however, on the general development of schemata for children's human figure drawings (see, for example, Lowenfeld, 1947; Goodnow, 1977; Freeman, 1980). Two main schemata have been distinguished: the tadpole schema and what, after Freeman (1980), we can term the "conventional schema". To elaborate, the tadpole schema is the basis for nearly all children's early human figure drawings. These drawings (see Figure 1) somewhat resemble tadpoles, hence their name. They consist of one central circle with, in many cases, facial features and legs. Arms are included less often than legs (Freeman, 1980). Between the ages of four and five years, many children start to portray a separate head and trunk in their drawings of the human figure and we can see evidence for the adoption of the conventional schema. Perhaps the most impressive evidence for children's reliance on schemata comes from studies in which they have been asked to draw unfamiliar topics. Many authors have noted that in such circumstances children will often use as their starting point the schema for a more familiar topic, which is then adapted to a greater or lesser extent to the new topic (see Figure 11.a). Freeman (1980), Goodnow (1977) and Graewe (1935) have all reported that children's drawings of an animal may often resemble their drawings of a human figure. Such similarity could arise if both types of drawings had evolved from a common "ancestor", such as the first enclosed form drawn by a child (the primordial circle; see Arnheim, 1956). Silk and Thomas (1986) studied drawings of a man and a dog made by 360 young children and concluded, however, that it was more likely that the animal drawings were adaptations of the schema for a drawing of a man. None of the man drawings contained dog features, although many dog drawings contained man features. Furthermore, several of the children rejected their first attempt at a dog drawing as too man-like ("It's turned out to be a man!"). Another manifestation of schema adaptation has been noted by Silk (1986) in a study of children's attempts at the unfamiliar task of drawing a man laying down.

Cues for alignment

For any drawing with two or more elements, a crucial problem is the alignment and positioning of the parts of the drawing on the page. Most adults take for granted that children will align their drawings with the edges of the paper and that the top of the drawing will be located towards the top of the page. Goodnow (1972) has provided a necessary reminder that children may not automatically regard the top of a page as being "higher" than the bottom of the page. If a child drawing on paper placed on a flat table, then the convention that the top of the page is the top of the scene or topic depicted requires a translation between up and down vertically in the picture and near and far horizontally on the page. The issue is further complicated if position on the page is also used to signal distance from the viewer, as in a perspective projection. The important point is that we should not take too much for granted and establish empirically exactly what cues children do use to position and align their drawing.

Turning now to the specifics of organizing and positioning the elements of a drawing, we find that there are three classes of cue which a child might use for this purpose. First, a child could use him/herself as a reference – thus each of the elements in a drawing could be oriented with respect to distance from a (stationary) child and to his/her left or right. Second, a child might orient each successive element of a drawing with respect to the elements already drawn. Finally, a child could orient the elements with respect to the wider context of the paper on which the drawing is made. Let us consider children's use of each of these cues in turn.

Influence of relative position of drawer

Children at the scribbling stage, around two years of age, often seem oblivious to the orientation of their drawing on the page. Furthermore, many authorities (e.g. Kellogg, 1970) have noted that such "basic" scribbling frequently appears to be executed without visual guidance. Clearly, any drawing made without eye control must be oriented solely with respect to the drawer. Older children, who often rely on other cues, may also still orient some of their drawing with respect to themselves. Freeman (1980), for example, has reported that in some circumstances the main (vertical) axis of children's human figure drawings can be oriented simply by the children drawing the pencil towards themselves, regardless of the placement of the drawing paper. Kennedy (1974, 1980) discusses the evidence that totally blind people can nevertheless perceive, recognize and produce line drawings. (The drawings are made of raised lines on sheets of plastic film and are perceived by touch.) These pictorial skills are likely often to involve orientation of lines with respect to the position of the blind drawer/ perceiver. Thus, it seems reasonable to conclude that drawings can be, and often are, oriented with respect to the drawer; but the extent to which children rely on their own position as a cue to orient their drawing has not yet been clearly established.

Influence of local visual cues

As a child works on a drawing, the parts already completed present new stimuli which may influence the position and orientation of later parts of the drawing. In making a drawing of a human figure, most children start by drawing the outline of the head. It is self-evident that in subsequent positioning of eyes, nose and mouth, most children of four years and older will position these features in relation to the outline of the head. For many children the next step in drawing the figure will be to add the trunk and legs. Goodnow and Friedman (1972) suggest that the trunk and legs in younger children's drawings will be aligned perpendicular to the axis of the eyes rather than to the baseline provided by the lower edge of the paper. Thus, if by chance the axis of the eyes should be drawn tilted with respect to the paper, then the main axis of the head and trunk should end up tilted as well (see Figure 2.c). Hargreaves (reported in Freeman, 1980) has confirmed this suggestion by asking children to complete a picture in which a head with deliberately tilted eyes had been pre-drawn by the experimenter. Careful analysis of the orientation of the subsequently drawn trunk and legs confirmed that the tilt of the eye axis significantly affected the orientation of the rest of the figure.

Another intriguing instance of control by local cues from a part-completed drawing concerns the positioning of the arms. In the human figure drawings in Figure 2.b, the arms appear to have been drawn coming out of the side of the head. This is not a symptom of a seriously disturbed conception, indeed it is quite common for children to make drawings with the arms attached to the head. The explanation offered by Freeman and Hargreaves (1977) and Freeman (1980) is that, in choosing a point of attachment for the arms, children commonly tend to attach them to the largest of the already drawn body segments. In a visually correct projection of the head and trunk, the result of this tendency would be the (correct) attachment of the arms to the trunk. We have already seen, however, that children often overestimate the size of the head relative to that of the trunk (for reasons connected with the planning and sequencing of the drawing task). Where the head is actually drawn larger than the trunk (a common occurrence even in the drawings made by children as old as five years), then the application of the above positioning rule will lead to the attachment of the arms on the head. Children's reliance on the relative size of body segments in positioning the arms can be clearly seen if they are provided with pre-drawn circles of varying sizes to represent the head and trunk. Freeman and Hargreaves (1977) and Freeman (1980) found a reliable tendency among two- to four-year-old children to position the arms onto the largest segment regardless of whether it stood for the head or the trunk. This effect, termed "the body-proportion effect", was more pronounced among tadpole drawers than among conventional drawers who had progressed to drawing a differentiated head and trunk in their spontaneous free drawings of a human figure.

Influence of contextual cues

The extent to which children use (or fail to use) the edges of the paper to align their drawing has important implications for Piaget's theories of the child's conception of space. This is so because the problems to be solved in locating and aligning elements of a drawing on paper are similar to those encountered in locating objects in space (Piaget and Inhelder, 1956). Indeed, as we have noted above (Chapter 1), Piaget seems to have regarded children's drawings very much as convenient illustrations of their comprehension of three-dimensional space (see Chapters 4 and 6).

While the location of objects in three-dimensional space may seem obvious and natural to adults, Piaget argued that the ability to organize space in terms of a co-ordinate reference system is one of the more significant achievements in children's cognitive development. In terms of Piaget's theory, the conception of a general co-ordinate reference system provides a context or framework in which any given set of objects can be arranged. Children younger than seven years of age will normally not have attained such a conception of space and their performance on a variety of spatial tasks will be marked by a number of characteristic errors. In Figure 15.a, for example, the positioning of the chimney perpendicular to the sloping outline of the roof, rather than to the horizontal baseline of the drawing, is common in drawings of children younger than seven years of age. This misalignment of the chimney is explained by Piaget as a consequence of the child's lack of comprehension of the vertical. A lack of understanding of the horizontal is proposed by Piaget as the cause of children's failure to predict or copy correctly the surface of the liquid in a tilted container (see Figure 15.b). Children aged between four and seven years typically represent the surface of the liquid at right angles to the outline of the tilted container.

Much recent research, including research into children's drawing, suggests that the reason why many young children fail to orient the surface of the liquid correctly is not because they lack a conception of the horizontal, but because of a performance bias in which local cues predominate. Ibbotson and Bryant (1976) have attributed the tilted flask error to a perpendicular bias – a tendency for children to draw intersecting lines at right angles to each other. Bremner (1985) has argued that many of the results cited in support of a perpendicular bias are also consistent with an alternative interpretation – that children tend to draw the intersecting line to produce a more symmetrical figure. One study by Bremner and Taylor (1982) required children to copy the shapes shown in Figure 16. The results confirmed that children are biased towards making symmetrical bisections rather than making right angles (as predicted by the hypothesis of a perpendicular bias).

The extent to which children use each kind of cue (self, local features or context) is also relevant to Piaget's theory. Sole use of the self as a reference is claimed by Piaget to be characteristic of young children's thinking in general, which he describes as egocentric thinking. The demonstration that young children were sometimes sensitive to context in aligning their drawings would, therefore, be evidence against Piaget's account. Clear evidence for sensitivity to context has been provided in the study by Hargreaves (see Freeman, 1980) in which children were asked to complete a figure of a man in which the head had been pre-drawn. As noted above, the orientation of the axis of the eyes was found to influence the orientation of the axis of the trunk added by the child. Crucially for the present discussion, the orientation of the eye axis *in relation to the page* was also important, with even six-year-old children showing a significant tendency towards aligning the figure with the edge of the paper.

Summary

It is only recently that psychologists have come to recognize that drawing is a complex activity for children. With this recognition has come the realization that the drawing process can make an important contribution to the finished picture. In the process of making a picture, children encounter planning, positioning and alignment problems. Their solutions to these problems may be subject to perceptual and performance biases. Only when all these factors have been considered and allowed for can we begin to interpret drawings for what they might reveal of children's conceptions and feelings.

6 What information is presented in a drawing?

The question of the information contained in a drawing lies at the heart of psychologists' attempts to understand and explain children's drawing. In this chapter we shall be chiefly concerned with information about the structure and appearance of the topic or scene represented in a drawing, rather than with children's feelings or emotions about the topic portrayed. (We shall discuss the emotional dimension in Chapter 7.) For our present interest it is essential to be clear from the outset about the kinds of information a drawing can present.

Some drawings are purely symbolic in the sense proposed by Goodman (see Chapter 3), that is to say, they denote the topic but do not resemble or convey information about it. First drawings made by children are often thought to be of this symbolic nature and are discussed briefly below.

Drawings that present information about the topic or scene portrayed can provide us with two types of information. Marr (1982), in his work on vision, made the distinction between these two types of information very clearly and forcefully. He distinguished between information about the structure of an object or scene and information about the way that object or scene looks from a particular viewpoint. Pictures that present structural information can be further subdivided into those that provide information about the structure of the object (often termed *object-centred* representations) and those that present information about the spatial relations of objects in a scene (often termed *array-centred* representations). Pictures that present information about the way an object or scene looks from a particular viewpoint are often termed *viewer-centred* representations. An important point about viewer-centred representations is that, depending on the particular viewpoint selected, they may not necessarily be good for conveying structural information about the object and the scene.

We need now to look in more detail at the presentation of these different kinds of information and consider factors that can influence information presentation. Most of children's free drawing is from memory; we have discussed in Chapter 4 the kinds of topic children normally choose to portray. Analysis of the information intended and presented in drawings, however, has required an analysis of specific tasks (such as drawing a model cube), which are not usually part of children's drawing experiences.

Symbolic drawings

Some of the very early drawings made by young children seem to function principally as conventional symbols that denote rather than describe the topics which they represent. In consequence, these early drawings often convey very little information about the structure or appearance of their referent. The first dog drawings of young children, for example, are often scarcely modified versions of the children's graphic formula for a human figure (see Figure 11.a).

The conventional symbolic character of much of young children's drawing can also be clearly seen in a study carried out by Barrett and Light (1976). In this study children were asked to make a drawing of a model house which had several distinctive features: there was no door, the upper windows were larger than the lower and there were curtains in the windows. Many of the five-year-old children failed completely to portray these distinctive features in their drawing of this model, but rather drew a standard schematic house (often a front view showing a door with a window on either side). According to Barrett and Light (1976), young children start by making generic drawings – they depict the genus to which the drawing topic belongs rather than any one individual exemplar. This stage, they suggest, could be described as symbolic realism. Generic drawings convey information at most about some of the defining characteristics of the class of things to which the drawing topic belongs.

Object-centred information

Many investigators, from Luquet onwards, have noted that young children often seem very concerned to present information about the salient characteristics and structure of an object in their drawing. The features of children's drawing most commonly cited as evidence for this concern include children's predilection for canonical views and the occurrence of transparency drawings. Luquet (1927) referred to these characteristics as intellectual realism. As we shall see, however, the evidence must be interpreted with care.

Canonical representation

Hochberg used the term "canonical form" to describe that view of an object that best displays its characteristic features (Hochberg, 1978, p. 195). Freeman (1980) has since used the term "canonical representation" to refer to general-purpose representations that make the object easily recognizable. The canonical representation of a house or a human figure, for example, is usually a front view; that of a car or a fish is normally a side view (see Figure 17). The canonical view of an object is the best view for conveying structural information (Freeman, 1980, p. 346).

That children consistently choose to draw familiar objects in their canonical orientation has frequently been pointed out (e.g. Freeman and Janikoun, 1972; Goodnow, 1977). When Ives and Rovet (1979) asked two- to twelve-year-old children to draw a man, a house, an owl, a horse, a car and a boat, they found that canonical views were adopted in nearly all cases. The man, house and owl were drawn in a front view by large numbers of children in all age groups. Drawings of a horse, car and boat, however, were nearly always represented in a side view, at least by the older children. Ives and Rovet (1979) concluded that children frequently rely on standard orientations when they are drawing. In a subsequent study, Ives (1980) showed that young children's preference for canonical orientations persisted even when they were asked to draw topics presented in different orientations.

A study conducted by Freeman and Janikoun (1972) is of

special interest here, because it shows that children's preference for canonical representations is not just a matter of executive limitations. Freeman and Janikoun found that, up to the age of about seven years, children prefer to draw canonical views even on tasks where it is clear that the production of another (non-canonical) view is within their capabilities. In this study five- to nine-year-old children were presented with a cup, which they were asked to draw. The cup was shown in a non-canonical orientation, so that the handle (a defining feature of cups) could not be seen. A painted flower (a non-defining feature) was, however, clearly visible on the outside of the cup facing the children. The children were asked to draw what they could see. A drawing of the cup in its canonical orientation would include the hidden handle. All that was required for the production of a non-canonical view, therefore, was the omission of the handle. The five- to seven-year-old children included the hidden handle and omitted the visible flower, whereas the eight- to nine-year-old children drew the flower and omitted the handle. This result means that the younger children chose to present structural information about the object by including a defining feature (the handle) of the cup even though it was out of view. The older children, however, included only the visible features of the object regardless of whether or not these were defining features, thus presenting view-specific information (in accord with the experimenter's instructions).

The conclusion that children up to the age of seven years are disposed to include object-centred structural information at the expense of view-specific information is reinforced by studies which have manipulated the amount of information about the structure made available to the child. Bremner and Moore (1984, Experiment 1) asked five- to seven-year-old children to draw a mug with a handle and a block with a spike sticking out on one end. The objects were positioned so that these features were not actually visible to the children when they made their drawings. The investigators found that children allowed to view the objects from various angles prior to drawing were more likely to make canonical drawings showing these defining features than children who had not pre-viewed the objects (see also Moore, 1987).

Size-scaling within an object

One potentially important aspect of the structure of many complex objects is the relative size of their various components. As we have seen in Chapter 5, children are sensitive to the relative sizes of head and trunk when they come to position the arms on a drawing of a human figure. Freeman and Hargreaves (1977) and Freeman (1980) present data that demonstrate that young children have a tendency to position the arms on the largest body element, whether this is the trunk or head. Can we expect, then, that children will be disposed to produce the parts of a drawing in their correct relative sizes?

Many authorities in the past have asserted that children up to six years of age do not scale the parts of their drawings accurately (Lowenfeld, 1939; Barkan, 1955; Arnheim, 1956). Size, it has often been suggested, reflects the importance of the topic (see Chapter 7). We have also found that planning problems and other performance factors may, for example, affect the relative sizes of head and trunk in children's human figure drawing (see Chapter 5). Nevertheless, recent evidence indicates that we may have seriously underestimated children's intentions to produce correct scaling in their drawing.

Thomas and Tsalimi (1988), for example, found that the common tendency of children to exaggerate the size of the head in relation to the trunk was the result of a planning failure. Specifically, children usually draw the head before the trunk and then fail to leave sufficient space for a visually correct depiction of the rest of the figure. When this planning difficulty was reduced, by telling the children to draw the trunk before the head, accurately scaled drawings were obtained, even from very young children.

The supposition that children have visually realistic intentions with regard to size scaling is reinforced by a study by Allik and Laak (1985), who suggested that size may be a characteristic of the canonical representation of an object which children have in their minds. Allik and Laak furthermore found that the size consistency was maintained when the drawing task was repeated and that a relative size consistency was maintained when the drawing task itself was changed (from free drawing to completion drawing). The latter finding suggests, according to

Allik and Laak, that children are operating a rule whereby a small head goes with a small body and a large head goes with a large body. What is drawn on paper is drawn in proportion to what is already there, and this is not affected by the order in which these items are drawn, but rather by the content of the topic. Thus, in drawing a human figure, children are directed in their proportioning of the body parts by the principle that the head must be smaller than the body.

Transparencies

Freeman (1980) distinguishes between two types of transparency drawing. In the first type, like the drawing of a fly in the spider's stomach (Figure 5.a), there seems no reason to doubt the child's intention to show what is normally invisible. In the second type, the child fails to show occlusion of one thing hidden behind another. The drawing of the rider's leg through the body of the horse (Figure 5.b) is an example of this second type. Can the occurrence of transparency drawings of the second type also be taken as evidence for children's concern to present structural information?

In his classic study of this phenomenon, Clark (1987) asked children aged six to sixteen years of age to draw an apple with a hat pin stuck through it. He found an age-related tendency to draw a circle with a horizontal line right across it. It is tempting to conclude that the younger children drew the hidden portion of the hat pin in their drawing because of their interest in presenting structural information. There are, however, reasons for doubting this simple interpretation of this type of transparency drawing.

Crook (1984) investigated transparency drawings by asking children to draw a stick pushed through a ball, a task which is structurally similar to that used by Clark. Just like Clark, Crook found that the majority of young children (five-year-olds) drew the stick right across the ball. Crook then introduced two variants of the task, designed to increase the amount of information hidden inside the ball. In the first task, two short sticks were pushed into opposite sides of the ball so that they met in the middle. The visual appearance of the arrangement, therefore, was the same as before, but the children knew that there was a hidden join in the sticks. In the second variant of the task, a single stick painted black and red was pushed into the ball so that the join between the colours was hidden. Both these arrangements elicited fewer transparency drawings in comparison with the original task, despite concealing more information within the ball. If transparencies are prompted by a desire to inform, it seems very odd that increasing the information buried in the ball (the joins in the sticks) should actually result in fewer transparency drawings.

From his results, Crook (1984, 1985) argued that the stick and ball transparencies should not be considered as attempts to communicate structural information. Applying this conclusion more generally, it seems that we cannot always assume that because children present structural information in their drawing, they necessarily intend to communicate that information. Crook suggests that young children base their drawings on structural descriptions of the topic (see Chapter 5) and that the presentation of structural information is sometimes merely a by-product of this aspect of the drawing process.

Drawings of three-dimensional objects

Drawings of real objects involve the representation of three dimensions on the two dimensions of a flat surface. For many of the drawing topics so far discussed, there are few special problems in producing a recognizable two-dimensional drawing of the object. Drawing a human figure, for example, involves the representation of a three-dimensional solid body on two-dimensional paper. Such a drawing is relatively easy, partly because a recognizable and unambiguous canonical picture of a human figure can be constructed without representing depth. The same cannot be said of a drawing of a cube. The problem with drawing a cube is that a simple outline is ambiguous – it could be confused with a drawing of a flat surface. A canonical view of a cube requires the representation of depth so that the three-dimensional shape of the solid can be grasped. The cube, therefore, provides an excellent opportunity to study the progress towards portrayal of depth. The importance of research into drawings of a cube, according to Freeman (1986), is because the cube is the simplest rectilinear form which presents the problem of mapping many points (on the object) onto one point on the paper. To fully understand the problem, and children's attempts to solve it, we need to know something about projection systems for constructing pictures.

There has been a great amount of work on projection systems and their use in picture making (see, for example, Hagen, 1980a, 1985). We shall concentrate here on an influential account of children's use of projection systems by Willats (1977). According to Willats there are certain rules which children have to learn before they can draw three-dimensional relations on two-dimensional paper. These are rule systems which map spatial relationships in the scene into spatial relationships in the picture. Because these systems deal with the transformation of spatial relationships, Willats has termed them "transformation" systems. Willats considers four systems: orthographic, vertical oblique, oblique and perspective.

In the orthographic projection, "parallel rays strike the picture plane at right angles" (Willats, 1977, p. 80). An orthographic projection of a cube, for example, is a simple square which is the projection of one of the cube's sides when viewed at right angles (Figure 18.a). Orthographic projections do not provide information on depth.

In the vertical oblique projection, depth information is presented, but translated into the vertical dimension on the paper. "Parallel lines strike the picture plane at right angles in the horizontal plane, but at an oblique angle in the vertical plane" (Willats, 1977, p. 80). A vertical oblique projection of a cube consists of two rectangular segments, one above the other (Figure 18.b). The lower segment represents the front face of a cube viewed at right angles, the upper segment represents an oblique view of the top face of the same cube.

In the oblique projection, parallel rays strike the picture plane at any angle and edges in the third dimension of an object are presented by oblique lines. An oblique projection of a cube consists of three segments: a square front face and adjoining parallelograms representing the top and one side face (see Figure 18.c).

In the final projection system, as outlined by Willats – perspective projection – "the projection rays converge to a vanishing point on the picture surface" (1977, p. 81). The perspective projection corresponds to the photographically realistic representations studied by Selfe (1983) and is termed "artificial perspective" by Gibson (1979). Perspective projections differ from oblique projections in that picture elements diminish in size with increasing distance from the viewer. In consequence, all perspective projections of a cube which display more than a single face of the cube contain no right angles or parallel lines.

An oblique projection of a cube comes closest to being the canonical view of a cube. The oblique projection provides the most direct mapping of shapes and angles onto paper while still presenting depth information unambiguously. That is why, according to research by Hagen (1985), we find that oblique projections are preferred by many older children and adult drawers. (Hagen's term for an oblique projection is orthogonal projection.) Given that young children regularly display a canonical bias in their drawing, we might expect, therefore, that an oblique projection would be their preferred solution to the task of drawing a cube. However, an oblique projection seems likely to present young drawers with some special difficulties. It entails, for example, joining lines at oblique angles – an achievement that we know is difficult for young children who are susceptible to perpendicular and symmetrical biases(see Chapter 5).

It turns out that cubes are indeed difficult to draw (Cox, 1986b; Freeman, 1986) and prompt a great variety of different solutions. As Freeman notes, it is possible in some cases to interpret children's attempts to draw cubes in terms of the projection systems proposed by Willats. Some quite common types of cube drawing are not so easy to classify. An early type of cube drawing consists of a single square (consistent with an orthographic projection). Two-segment drawings (consistent with use of a vertical oblique projection) are also quite common. Older children may draw five squares in the form of a cross, to produce something which resembles an unfolded box (see Figure 18.d). Other solutions consist of rectangles crossed with lines. Children of nine years and older are more likely than younger ones to produce an oblique projection in which three sides of the cube are visible (Willats, 1977). Both Hagen (1985) and Willats (1985) report that perspective projections, with diminishing size with depth, are relatively rare even in the drawings of older adolescents and adults.

Note that interpretation of the intention behind a drawing is not always straightforward. Consider cube drawings which consist of a single square. Do the young children who often produce this solution intend the square to represent a single face of the cube, which implies the use of an orthographic projection to present view-specific information? Or is the square intended to represent the whole cube (as suggested by Arnheim, 1956)? Moore (1985) attempted to answer this question by asking children to draw a cube in which each face was marked with a different colour. When they had made their drawing, children who produced a single square were then given coloured pens and asked to add the colours. Seven-year-old children added more than one colour to the single square, indicating that for them it represented all the faces of the cube. The few older children who drew a single square always added only the colour of the front face of the cube, indicating that for them the square was an orthographic projection of the front face only.

To sum up, traditional assumptions about a developmental progression from object-centred to viewer-centred depictions break down when we consider children's attempts to draw a cube. To some extent this is because an object-centred, canonical depiction of a cube that adequately conveys depth information (an oblique projection) is difficult for young children to draw. It is interesting to note that even adults seem to prefer this projection, even though it does not accurately present the normal visual appearance of a real cube (as a perspective projection can). As Cox (1986b) has noted with regard to cube drawings, children often seem more visually realistic in their drawing, and adults less so, than traditional suppositions might lead one to believe.

Array-specific information

When children make drawings of more than one topic in isolation, then there is the possibility of presenting information about the relationships between the topics as well as information on individual topics. Array-specific information is information about the spatial arrangement of two or more objects in a scene. There is evidence that children are sensitive to such arrangements and try to convey information about spatial relationships in their drawings, even at the expense of view-specific information. A study by Light and Humphreys (1981) provides a nice demonstration of young children's concern to present array-specific information. In this study, children were asked to draw two model pigs, one painted red, the other green. The pigs were arranged so that the red pig was always following the green one. The children were then asked to draw this arrangement four times, each in a different orientation *vis-à-vis* the child. The resulting drawings from the five- and six-year-olds invariably contained information about the array (the red pig following the green one) but seldom any indication of the child's viewing position. Seven- and eight-year-olds' drawings were mostly view-specific (see below).

The presentation of array-specific information is straightforward for horizontal arrangements of one thing beside another – children generally draw the two objects side by side on the paper in a direct mapping of their horizontal relationship (see Figure 19). Drawing one thing behind another presents an altogether more severe test of the child's representational skills. The problem here is that there is no direct and easy projection of the third dimension of depth onto two-dimensional paper (see above). Freeman, Eiser and Sayers (1977) asked children to draw the outline of an apple in the middle of a sheet of paper and then to draw another apple behind it. There was a reliable tendency for most of the younger children (five- to seven-year-olds) to indicate something of the spatial arrangement by either drawing the apples side by side, or one above the other (Figure 19). With increasing age of drawer, there was a progressive shift from drawing the apples in a horizontal relation to drawing them in a vertical relation, with the more distant apple located higher up the page. View-specific information was frequent only in the drawings of older children, and almost always took the form of total or partial occlusion of the more distant apple (Figure 19). Interestingly, transparency drawings with interposition of the outlines of the two apples were extremely rare at all ages.

A recent study by Ingram and Butterworth (1989) has confirmed that transparency drawings are infrequent when children are asked to draw one thing behind another. In this study, children aged between three and eight years were asked to draw two blocks differing in size in various row and file arrangements. The major finding was that young children represented depth in the array vertically. Unlike Light and Humphreys (1981), however, Ingram and Butterworth found evidence that these vertical drawings of the file arrangement also contained view-specific information. Specifically, the further block was systematically located at the top of the picture, the blocks were drawn in a specific sequence and relative size differences were conveyed. It may be that having the two objects in the array clearly different (in terms of size) was a factor in eliciting view-specific information (see Cox, 1986a; and our discussion of view-specific information below).

Children's concern to represent accurately a rather different kind of spatial relationship – inside versus behind – is well demonstrated in a study by Light and MacIntosh (1980). In this study, children aged six to seven and a half years were asked to draw a model house placed either behind or inside a glass beaker. In the "inside" condition, all the children drew a house within the outline of the beaker. However, when the house was placed behind the beaker, about half the children drew the two items separately, that is, they drew the house and the beaker either next to or above each other. Clearly, then, these children were distinguishing between two conditions which looked the same (from the front), but which the children knew were different in their spatial configurations.

This study highlights an interesting facet of young children's concern to render array-specific information. Light and MacIntosh (1980) found that the area inside the drawn outline of the mug seems to be reserved for items that are located inside the real mug and not for things that are behind the mug and merely seen through it. This result implies that young children regard the area enclosed by a drawn outline as the boundary of the whole object and not as the occluding contour of the visible part of the object. This conclusion is reinforced by the results obtained by Moore (1985), discussed in the previous section. She found that seven-year-olds consider that a square drawn to represent a cube stands for the whole cube and not just the front face (see above).

The implied convention that inside the outline signifies inside the object may explain why Freeman and Janikoun (1972) found that the five- to seven-year-olds omitted to draw a flower painted on the outside of a teacup which they had been asked to draw (see above). If inside the drawn outline of the cup was reserved for items actually in the cup then these children had no easy solution to the placement of the flower (see Taylor and Bacharach, 1982). Willats (1985, p.90) has noted that drawing the seam on the surface of a ball presents some young children with a similar dilemma. To the extent that four- to five-year-old children tend to regard an outline as the boundary of the whole object and not just an occluding contour, then their positioning of additional picture elements in relation to this contour confirms that array-specific information, like object-centred information and canonical representations, generally takes precedence over view-specific information.

View-specific information

We have already had cause to refer to view-specific information in order to distinguish it from array-specific and object-centred information. It may be helpful, however, to return to basics and start with a definition. View-specific information in a picture is information that conveys something about the position of the drawer/viewer in relation to the objects or scenes depicted. Pictures with a single viewing perspective or station point have become widespread in Western art, but other cultures have often developed styles in which several viewpoints are included within a single picture – for example, the art of Ancient Egypt and some kinds of primitive art.

When we consider children's drawing, there are two main ways in which a picture can convey view-specific information: first, the aspect of the topic depicted gives information on the orientation of the topic with respect to the viewer; second, the occlusion of one object behind another gives information on the viewer's line of sight and hence their position. There are, of course, additional view-specific properties of a real scene, such as foreshortening and diminishing size with distance, which can be captured in a perspective projection (see above). Perspective projections, however, are a late accomplishment for only a few children and relatively rare even in the drawings made by adults.

Let us first consider orientation of a drawing as a way of signalling viewing position. Young children, we have seen, have a tendency to draw objects in their canonical orientation regardless of viewing position. Freeman and Janikoun (1972) found that children up to the age of seven years drew the handle on the side of a cup, despite the fact that the cup was turned so that the handle could not be seen from the child's viewpoint. Eight-year-old children, however, did provide view-specific information by omitting the hidden handle from their drawings.

Are children younger than seven years unalterably object-centred in their drawing or can they be induced to present view-specific information? It is possible that the absence of view-specific information in drawings made by these children reflects their conceptual immaturity (see Piaget and Inhelder, 1956), in which case no amount of tinkering with the details or presentation of the task should make any difference. On the other hand, if lack of view-specific information reflects lack of concern rather than lack of cognitive ability, then restructuring the drawing task to make viewpoint more salient might be enough to elicit view-specific drawings from younger children.

One possible way to make the orientation of a cup more salient for young children is to present them with "scene contrast" as Davis (1983) has shown. Like Freeman and Janikoun, she presented four- to seven-year-old children with a cup turned so that the handle could not be seen, and like Freeman and Janikoun she found that the children drew the cup in its canonical orientation showing the (hidden) handle on the side. Davis then found that adding a second cup with the handle visible to the child, helped the five- to six-year-old children to produce view-specific drawings of the first cup (i.e. they now omitted the hidden handle). The four-year-old children, however, still produced canonical representations of the target cup and did not show the contextual sensitivity found in the drawings of the older children.

A similar sensitivity to the presentation of the task has been found in children's drawings of one thing behind another. In such an arrangement, view-specific information is conveyed by the total or partial occlusion of the more distant object by the nearer one. As we have noted, Freeman, Eiser and Sayers (1977) asked children aged between five and ten years to draw one apple behind another. Nine- and ten-year-olds typically drew the apples so that the nearer one partially occluded the further. Most of the younger children drew the two apples as separate and non-overlapping. Cox (1981) used an essentially similar arrangement but tried to emphasize viewpoint in order to encourage younger children to show occlusion. Cox based her design on a suggestion by Donaldson (1978) and incorporated the notion of "hiding" in a "cops and robbers" task. In this task, a game was acted out using models of a robber, a policeman and a wall. Four- to ten-year-old children were told that the policeman was chasing the robber, who hid behind the wall, but whose head was still visible to the policeman over the wall. The children were asked to draw what the policeman could see or, in a second condition, what they themselves could see when acting out the role of the policeman. The drawings by the majority of the children aged six and above represented the scene using partial occlusion. Surprisingly, nearly half the number of four-year-old children also showed partial occlusion in their draw-ings, which led Cox to conclude that young children *are* able to make view-specific drawings in favourable circumstances.

If four-year-olds can be induced to show occlusion, then their normal failure to do so cannot be attributed to conceptual immaturity. In that case, what was the important feature of Cox's procedure that encouraged view-specific drawings? It may have been important that the occluding element (the wall) and the occluded element (the robber) were different types of thing. In other studies of occlusion these two elements have often been the same – for example, one apple behind another apple (as in Freeman *et al.*, 1977). In a subsequent study by Cox (1985), children who were asked to draw one ball "hiding" behind another ball produced far fewer partial occlusions compared to those found with the man behind the wall in the cops and robbers task. Neither the notion of hiding nor turning the task into a game, therefore, seemed to elicit more view-specific representations (see also Light and Simmons, 1983). What *did* seem to affect the number of partial occlusions was the occluded object itself, with the man resulting in the highest rates of occlusion (see also Light and Foot, 1986). Cox (1986a) concluded, therefore, that children (aged six years) were more likely to portray partial occlusion if the two objects were very different and to fail to do so if the objects were similar. However, for young children (aged four years) all conditions resulted in a very small number of partial occlusions. For this age group, highly contextualized tasks in addition are required to elicit partial occlusion (see above). According to Cox (1986a), the degree of similarity of the two objects affects the number of partial occlusions because it influences the extent to which children look at the arrangement to be drawn. She suggests that if two objects are very similar, then the children will not need to return to the model after having drawn the first object. When the two objects are very different, on the other hand, children may have to return to the model in order to refresh their mental image of the second object and consequently may be more likely to become aware that only part of it is visible. As a result, more visually realistic pictures emerge.

Turning now to a wider issue, we have found that in appropriate circumstances even four-year-olds may present view-specific information in their drawings. We may reasonably conclude, therefore, that the frequently noted absence of view-specific information in young children's free drawing is not a product of a conceptual limitation. In this connection, it is worth remembering that adults are often less visually realistic in their drawing than has sometimes been assumed (see, for example, Willats, 1977; Hagen, 1985; Cox, 1986b).

Size-scaling between objects

Another kind of relational information is the size scaling between objects in a picture. As we have seen, children's use of perspective projections with diminishing size with distance is relatively rare. In the relative scaling within an object, young children convey structural information about the size of the different elements of that object (see above). Can we assume that size differences between objects in a picture reflect children's attempts at visually correct size scaling? Previously it has been claimed (e.g. Barkan, 1955; Arnheim, 1956) that with regard to size scaling, young children start with an undifferentiated phase, in which the sizes of the different topics are not important and, therefore, that the size they are drawn will not be visually realistic. Where size is important – for example, in drawing a man standing in a doorway – children may make some attempt at differentiation of the topics, but accurate proportions are seldom portrayed. When in older children's drawings size is eventually differentiated, according to Arnheim, it starts first within one object and only later does accurate size scaling between objects emerge.

However, we have carried out some research recently (Silk, 1986; Silk and Thomas, 1986, 1988) that suggests that young children *can* portray size scaling – at least, when size is an easy and salient dimension for differentiation. In the first of our studies (Silk and Thomas, 1986), we found that children as young as three-and-a-half-years-old produced appropriate ordinal scaling of heights in their drawings of a man and a dog. The majority of even the youngest children drew men taller than dogs, although even the six-and-a-half-year-olds somewhat overestimated the height of the dog. This finding is further illustrated in the drawings of house, man and dog in Figure 11. Although completely accurate size scaling is not achieved in these pictures, they show none the less that houses are taller than people who, in turn, are taller than dogs.

Why is it that we have found evidence of correct ordinal size scaling in children's drawings, whereas examples of incorrect scaling are apparently so numerous that some authorities have minimized children's abilities in this matter? Without doubt the size of a drawing may be affected by many other factors besides the real size of the topics portrayed. The importance of the topic (see Chapter 7) and the process of constructing a drawing (see Chapter 5) may all significantly modify the size of a drawing. Nevertheless, where these influences are not overwhelming, size of figure may offer an easy way for children to achieve distinguishable drawings of differently-sized topics. In Figure 11.a, for example, the most obvious difference between the drawings of house, man and dog is their relative size.

Consequently, we might expect that correct ordinal size scaling between topics will be less likely when size is not such a salient dimension and other features offer a ready way to distinguish the topics. This conclusion is supported by a further study (Silk and Thomas, 1988) in which we investigate the scaling of a man and a door on a pre-drawn house. Decreasing the distance between the man and door resulted in the children increasingly scaling the two objects more realistically. Thus it seemed that the relevant size of the topics did play a part for the children in their drawing and that when the man and the door were drawn closer on paper, this facilitated the comparison for the child, thus resulting in the closest match to visually realistic size scaling.

It seems that children as young as four years are capable of conveying on paper information regarding their knowledge of the sizes of certain topics. Although completely accurate sizes are seldom portrayed, young children nevertheless produce correct ordinal size scaling. The drawings appear to be based on a rule like "the man is larger than the dog" and "the house is larger than the man". Allik and Laak (1985) have analysed scaling within a figure in terms of the application of a rather similar rule (see above).

Conclusions

The information presented in a drawing seems to be determined by three factors: children's knowledge of the drawing topic itself, their interpretation of what aspects of that information are important to present and their capacity to produce a drawing showing that information. There has been a general tendency in the past to ignore or underestimate the importance of the last two factors. Thus, several traditional theoretical approaches (e.g. Luquet, 1927; Piaget and Inhelder, 1956; Harris, 1963) suggested that children's drawings principally reflect their state of conceptual and intellectual development. It is clear on questioning, however, that children often know more than their drawings reveal.

Gardner (1980), for example, reported how his six-year-old daughter, in her human figure drawings, would usually position the arms coming horizontally out of the middle of the body. In conversation she made it clear that she knew that arms really emanated from the shoulder and she had no difficulty in repositioning the arms correctly when requested to do so. In subsequent drawings, however, she once again reverted to her old choice of drawing the arms coming out of the middle of the body, commenting that that was how she liked to draw the arms.

As we have seen, drawing certain topics (such as a cube) presents particular problems which may be beyond the capacity of many younger children to resolve. Thus, we find that children's drawings of a cube may be a poor guide to their conception of spatial relations or their knowledge of rectilinear solids.

We can see that inferences about children's knowledge and concepts from the information in their drawings need to be made with care. Admittedly, the data so far available do not allow us to tell a tidy and complete story. There are still many gaps in our understanding of children's graphic intentions. But some tentative conclusions are possible.

Traditional assumptions about children's progression from intellectual realism to visual realism seem now to be an oversimplification. We have discussed many studies in which structured drawing tasks have elicited pictorial responses from children which they would not necessarily include in their free drawings. The context, content and instructions of the drawing task were found often to have an important effect on the children's drawing. In general, this chapter showed that recent research has indicated that young children in the stage of intellectual realism are capable of presenting much more information than was previously thought possible. As Freeman has stated: "it is undeniable that the under-sevens have been grossly underestimated until very recently" (1987, p. 148).

Much of what had been previously considered to be evidence for conceptual limitations has now been found to arise from executive difficulties or preferences for certain kinds of pictures. There does seem to be a general preference among children younger than seven years for drawings which convey information about the structure of the topic or the spatial relations of the array in which it is located. Older children often begin to make drawings that include view-specific information. The production of drawings of these various kinds does not always seem to be driven by a desire to inform or communicate, because attempts to turn drawing tasks into communication games have had only limited success at modifying children's drawings (see Cox, 1986a). It is tempting to conclude that the drawings characteristic of children's drawing development reflect what children at each stage typically regard as an adequate representation of the topic in question. Thus, for example, a five-year-old does not consider a drawing of a cup to be satisfactory unless you can see that the cup has a handle. Of course, children may accept in their own drawings mistakes or features that they would criticize in drawings of others. We should always remember the constraints placed on drawing production by the performance factors discussed in Chapter 5.

Accepting for the moment that children younger than seven years are disposed to make object-centred depictions and that older children tend to make viewer-centred drawings, we can now ask about the origins of these tendencies. There is no easy answer to this question yet available. As discussed in Chapter 3, Arnheim (1956) argued that there is a developmental basis to the usual progression and that in their perceptions as well as their drawing children start with the general structure of objects and only later do they become aware of the way an object looks from a specific viewpoint (see also Gibson, 1979). Some authorities, such as Hagen (1985), suggest that cultural influences may also be involved. Thus, for example, the tendency towards view-specific pictures in Western children's drawing may be due to the dominant ideal of visual realism in popular Western art.

Summary

Children in their drawings present different kinds of information. Early drawings may be no more than symbolic representations of the genus to which the drawing topic belongs. Later drawings often display object-centred information about the structure of the object depicted and (where appropriate) about the structure of the array of objects in the scene. Viewer-centred depictions are typically produced more frequently by children older than seven years. Performance factors often play a crucial role in determining the information apparently presented and must be recognised in any adequate attempt to draw inferences about children's knowledge and the kinds of information that they consider it important to present in their drawing.

7 Expressive aspects of drawing

In Chapter 6 we discussed the different kinds of information about structures and appearances of objects that children present in their drawings. We shall now consider whether or not these drawings also convey any emotional messages.

It is widely held that art is an expression of emotions and ideas as well as an attempt to produce a picture. Indeed, in some forms of adult art the communication of feeling may be more important than the production of a visually correct depiction. While trained artists may deliberately try to convey feeling, many psychologists have long believed that everyone, trained in art or not, may unconsciously express something of their emotional state when asked to draw or paint a picture. As long ago as 1876, in a study of imagination in madness, Simon noted a relation between the drawings and behavioural symptoms of severely disturbed patients. Goodenough (1926), although primarily concerned with the assessment of intelligence through drawings, noted that the analysis of children's drawings might also be of use for evaluating the children emotionally.

Looking back to these early beginnings we can now identify three distinct traditions of research into the emotional-expressive aspects of children's drawings. First came the analysis of drawings as projections of personality character-istics, interpreted mainly within the theoretical framework of psychoanalytic theory and its derivatives (Freud, 1976). The second research tradition, identified largely with the work of Elizabeth Koppitz (1968, 1984), comprises an attempt to devise and scientifically validate a classification of "emotional indi-cators" to be found in children's drawing. The third tradition has been concerned with discovering ways in which normal children depict personally important or emotionally significant topics, rather than with personality assessment or clinical diagnosis (see, for example, Sechrest and Wallace, 1964).

Projective interpretations of children's drawing

Work in this projective tradition has always been primarily clinical in orientation. Much of the research carried out within this tradition has consisted only of the analysis and reporting of individual cases (but see Hammer, 1958). From the 1930s, several clinicians have explored the clinical possibilities of projective drawings (see, for example, Schilder, 1935; Bender, 1938). The House-Tree-Person projective test, for example, requires the child to draw a house, a tree and a person; the resulting drawing is interpreted on the assumption that each item will function as a symbol for some emotionally important aspect of the child's life and experience (Buck, 1948). According to Hammer (1958), the house is capable of symbolizing the child's body, the womb or the parental home. The tree, it is claimed, is likely to reflect children's relatively deeper and more unconscious feelings about themselves. The person conveys children's conscious view about themselves and their relations with the rest of the world.

Perhaps the most influential of these early workers, however, was Karen Machover (1949), whose work on human figure drawings is still regarded by many as a definitive guide to projective interpretation of drawings. Machover produced a figure drawing test, now often called the "Draw-a-person" test. The subject is given a blank sheet of paper (preferably A4 size) and a soft lead pencil with an eraser. The subject is then asked to "draw a person". An alternative wording for very young children is to ask them to "draw somebody". While the subject makes the drawing, the tester should note the sequence of parts drawn and any points and questions raised by the subject. When this drawing is complete, the subject is given a fresh sheet of paper and asked to draw the opposite sex with a request, "now draw a man", or "now draw a woman" as appropriate.

Machover's analysis of the resulting drawings are largely based on the presumption that a child projects his/her self-image into his/her drawings of a human figure. Machover regarded drawings as expressions of the more permanent and enduring aspects of the child's personality rather than expressions of temporary emotional states. The choice of the sex of the first-drawn figure, Machover claimed, reflects the subject's primary sex-role identification. Scoring of the details of the drawings is essentially qualitative; the tester tries to build up a personality description of the subject from an analysis of the various features of the drawings. In common with psychoanalytic interpretations of other aspects of human activity, Machover's analysis of drawing allows for disguised and symbolic expressions of ideas, as well as their open and explicit depiction. A few examples from work in this tradition will help illustrate these points.

Virtually all authorities on the interpretation of projective drawing agree that the size of the drawing of the human figure is most significant, directly reflecting the drawer's own self-esteem (Buck, 1948; Machover, 1949; Hammer, 1958; Koppitz, 1968, 1984; Di Leo, 1970). Larger-than-average figures may be a sign of personality features such as aggression or grandiosity. Tiny drawings, much smaller than average for the relevant age group, may indicate inadequacy, inferiority, low self-esteem, anxiety or depression. This apparently simple equation of figure size with self-esteem, however, cannot be sustained even in the terms of psychoanalytic theory. A large human figure drawing may also be a product of feelings of inadequacy, in which case a large drawing reflects compensatory defences (Hammer, 1958). We should also note the reported tendency for black children living in the southern parts of the United States to make very large human figure drawings which are crowded up against the edges of the drawing paper (Hammer, 1958). In this context, large human figure drawings restricted by the size of the paper were claimed to express the frustration and restrictions experienced by blacks living in a society in which colour prejudice was widespread.

Many of the interpretations suggested for children's drawings relate to Freud's ideas about sexuality as a universal component of human motivation. Thus we find, for example, that depictions of the nose and thumbs are often interpreted as having phallic significance - this could be indicative of castration anxieties (Schildkrout, Shenker and Sonnenblick, 1972). Drawings in which the mouth has been emphasized (Figure 20) are often interpreted as expressions of orality (concern with oral gratification - often related to compulsive eating and dieting). Omission of the mouth can also be held to be expressive of concern with oral gratification - conceivably the denial of impulses to over-eat.

It is often proposed that the depiction of long arms and large hands (Figure 7.c) is expressive of power and control (Machover, 1949; Di Leo, 1970; Schildkrout *et al.* 1972); conversely, the omission of hands and/or arms is claimed to reflect feelings of powerlessness and ineffectuality. Human figure drawings in which the hands are placed in pockets or drawn behind the back are stated to express guilt and anxiety about controlling "forbidden" impulses. Among other factors used in the interpretation of projective drawing are the position of the drawing on the paper, shading and line thickness, sequence of parts drawn, extent and distribution of detailing, erasures and the depiction of clothing and background.

These interpretations are not presented as unvarying principles. Thus, for example, Schildkrout *et al.* (1972) present several human figure drawings (made by adolescents) in which the body is shown in front view but the face is drawn in profile (see Figure 21). This configuration is most often interpreted as indicative of defensive avoidance. Nevertheless, in other cases the same configuration is interpreted as an expression of rebelliousness; in yet another case this same configuration is found in a drawing which is stated to express self-confidence. It is common in books on the projective interpretation of drawings to find warnings that no single drawing or feature of a drawing should be taken in isolation, but that interpretations should only be made in the light of all the clinical evidence available.

The validity of projective drawing tests concerns the extent to which the interpretation of the drawings gives the same result as other independent assessments of the subject's personality or emotional state (but see Freeman, 1976). It is common to find claims that interpretations have been validated against clinical experience, but we are seldom given any independent evidence of the validity (or reliability) of these interpretations. Machover (1949), in her original presentation of her figure drawing test, reported that her work was based on a "substantial file of drawings" and that some small-scale studies had been conducted to assess the accuracy with which clinicians could match drawings and case records. Subsequent studies have yielded mixed results. Anastasi (1976) has concluded that the better controlled of the studies give no support for the personality interpretations proposed by Machover (see, for example, Roback, 1968; Swensen, 1957, 1968). To some extent this lack of support for projective drawing tests should be seen in a wider context, namely the generally poor performance of projective personality tests when assessed in adequately controlled studies. Nunnally has concluded that "as a group, projective tests do not provide very valid measures of personality traits" (1978, p. 571).

In the cases in which some attempt has been made to make systematic comparisons with an appropriate control group, it is unusual to find any independent validation of many of the (psychodynamic) interpretations. Hammer (1953), for example, found that black children made large drawings crowded against the edge of the paper (see above). He claimed that these drawings reflected the frustration experienced by black children in a predominantly colour-prejudice society; but we cannot exclude the possibility that some other aspect of these children's experience was responsible for that particular characteristic of their drawing. Indeed, the size of their drawings could have little to do with their experiences of colour prejudice; and it is easy to think of alternative explanations. Large drawings, for example, could simply reflect the kind of art teaching (or lack of it) they had received, which would have been different from that offered to white children in the segregated schools of the time.

Another problem in validating many of the projective interpretations is that the features of drawings which are claimed to be of clinical significance are also known to be partly a function of normal drawing development. To take just one example, the omission of hands and arms is claimed to reflect feelings of helplessness. However, it is common for children younger than five years of age not to show arms and/or hands in their drawing. It is scarcely to be conceived that all four-year-old children suffer from feelings of helplessness and in consequence omit arms and hands from their human figure drawings. Freeman (1980) suggests that there is a kind of end-anchoring effect whereby the head and legs are more likely to be portrayed than the arms because they define the endpoints of the dominant vertical axis. Some authors have quite explicitly taken such developmental considerations into account (see Koppitz, 1968, 1984), but many do not appear to have done so. Machover, for example, did most of her work on drawings made by adolescents, but generalized her conclusions to drawings made by younger children without sufficient warning that the inclusion or omission of features should be considered in the light of the subject's general level of drawing development.

A rather similar point has been made by Swensen (1968), who points out that there is considerable evidence that better adjusted subjects tend to make drawings of higher quality, and that features which are likely to occur in better quality drawings (erasures, greater use of shading, greater variety of different kinds of line) are among those proposed by Machover to be expressive of conflicts. If conflicts do indeed tend to produce such features, then the occurrence of such features is confounded by the quality of the drawing itself, which in turn reflects the general emotional adjustment of the subject. Clearly, any assessment of these features of a drawing for possible psychodynamic significance must take account of the over-all quality of the drawing itself.

The reliability of projective drawing tests is also problematic. There are several dimensions to the question of reliability of a test based on drawings. First, there is the question of whether the drawings made by a subject are likely to display the same significant features on two different occasions of testing. If a subject produces drawings that vary a great deal, then it is not likely that any one drawing will be a reliable expression of that subject's personality. Second, given that the problems of obtaining a representative drawing from a subject have been overcome, then we can consider a projective drawing test to be reliable if two independent testers make similar personality interpretations from the same drawing. To agree on personality interpretations, the two testers will have to agree not only on the objective scoring of the features of the drawing (presence/absence of details, relative and absolute sizes and so forth), but also on the analysis and interpretation of the significance of those details. Commenting on drawing tests as a group, Harris (1963) noted that a number of studies have found that, in general, subjects show some consistency in their drawings over time and that there is fairly good agreement on the objective identification of details in drawings. As to the clinical interpretation of the features found in the drawings, we are not aware of any good evidence of substantial agreement between testers. Commenting on projective tests in general, Anastasi (1976) noted that the few adequately controlled studies that are available have revealed dramatic disagreements between different testers' interpretations of the same projective responses.

Given that personality interpretations of projective drawing are generally unreliable and invalid, it comes as quite a surprise to find that these figure-drawing tests are still very popular, particularly with clinicians. Anastasi (1976) points out that in practice they may be used less as a personality test, than as a clinical tool for facilitating discussion with a patient. Thus the administration of a projective test can serve to help "break the ice" at an initial clinical interview and provide a convenient framework within which initial discussion can take place. Drawing tests are usually extremely easy to administer and are often enjoyed by patients. In consequence, such tests provide a ready means of obtaining additional qualitative information about the patient. Anastasi concludes that projective tests may "serve best in sequential decisions, by suggesting leads for further exploration or hypotheses about the individual for subsequent verification" (1976, p. 587).

Emotional indicators in children's drawing

Elizabeth Koppitz offered us a very different approach to the emotional-expressive aspects of drawing from that developed earlier by Machover. Koppitz found Harry Stack Sullivan's Interpersonal Relationship Theory more useful in her work than the psychoanalytic framework adopted by Machover. Koppitz based her work on the assumption that human figure drawings "reflect primarily a child's level of development and his interpersonal relationships, that is, his attitudes toward himself and toward the significant others in his life" (Koppitz, 1968, p. 3). Koppitz assumed that current anxieties would also be expressed in the drawing, which she took to be a reflection more of current emotional states than of enduring personality characteristics or a "body image" (cf. Machover, 1949, above). For her human figure drawing test Koppitz relied on just one drawing collected from a child, rather than the two drawings required for Machover's "draw-a-person" test. Koppitz argued that the additional information to be gained from a second drawing does not justify the extra time required. In the Koppitz test, the tester gives the child a blank sheet of A4 size paper, a pencil and an eraser. The child is then instructed: "On this piece of paper, I would like you to draw a WHOLE person. It can be any kind of person you want to draw, just make sure that it is a whole person and not a stick figure or a cartoon figure" (Koppitz, 1968). Koppitz considered it important that the child makes the drawing in the presence of the examiner and considered individual testing to be preferable to group testing. The drawings are then scored according to Koppitz's system.

One of the strengths of Koppitz's approach over that of Machover is that Koppitz took into account the changes in children's drawings which are characteristic of normal drawing development. This is a crucial improvement because, as Koppitz herself pointed out, the presence or absence of a particular detail can be clinically significant at one age but not at another (see previous discussion of presence/absence of arms on children's human figure drawings).

In order to assess developmental changes in human figure drawings, Koppitz devised a classification of objectively defined developmental indicators. Koppitz considered as developmental indicators those features of human figure drawings that are rare in the drawings of young children and become increasingly common in the drawings of older children. The thirty items eventually selected were derived from the Goodenough-Harris scoring system and Koppitz's own clinical experience. The developmental items so identified generally cover limbs, facial detail and clothing. Koppitz undertook several studies that demonstrated that the occurrence of these items was primarily related to age and relatively independent of education and drawing ability. Koppitz (1968) presented normative data on the occurrence of the thirty developmental items for children aged five years to twelve years.

As a result of her researches and drawing on the work of Machover and Hammer, Koppitz (1968) also identified thirty emotional indicators that may be found in children's human figure drawings. These were items which:

1. occurred more often in the human figure drawings of disturbed children than in those of normal children;
2. were unusual in the human figure drawings of normal children;
3. were not related solely to age and maturation.

Examples of emotional indicators are: gross asymmetry of limbs, depiction of teeth, legs drawn pressed together, omission of certain facial details and omission of limbs.

Koppitz (1984) extended her analysis of emotional and developmental indicators to human figure drawings made by adolescents. For this older age group, Koppitz concluded (as have other investigators) that figure drawings are not as good a guide to intelligence and intellectual maturity as they are for younger children (see also Scott, 1981). She used the same emotional indicators for adolescents as for younger children, although she reports no normative data to justify this extension of her analysis. She also suggested that, for the older children, the interpretation of emotional indicators is most usefully performed when the indicators are grouped into five categories, reflecting impulsivity, insecurity, anxiety, shyness and anger, respectively. This classification of indicators was not, however, supported by data and statistical analysis in the rigorous way that the original analyses were (Koppitz, 1968). Indeed, we rather feel that in her later book Koppitz (1984) took a step backwards in scientific terms from the position of her earlier work (Koppitz, 1968). To be fair, Koppitz (1984) no longer presented her analysis of human figure drawing as a psychometric test, but rather as a clinical technique which, in combination with other methods, may help a clinician elicit information from a patient. She always stressed:

It is not possible to make a meaningful diagnosis or evaluation of a child's behaviour or difficulties on the basis of any single sign on a HFD. The *total* drawing and the combination of various signs and indicators should always be considered and should then be analyzed on the basis of the child's age, maturation, emotional status, social and cultural background and should then be evaluated together with other available test data. (Koppitz, 1968, p. 55)

A serious limitation to Koppitz's early work, however, is that she offered no theory of emotional expression in drawing to which the various developmental and emotional indicators could be related and which would serve to integrate her work. Her subsequent attempt (Koppitz, 1984) to introduce some integration of this kind by grouping emotional indicators into categories is of doubtful value; she presented no systematic data to validate the categories proposed and the accompanying interpretations are reminiscent of those proposed by Machover and by Hammer, which have been found to have very poor validity when assessed in adequately controlled studies.

To summarize, Koppitz has provided us with a list of items known to discriminate reliably between human figure drawings made by emotionally disturbed children and those made by normal children. Her interpretations of figure drawing thus possess a degree of empirical support which is lacking from previous attempts to assess the personalities and emotional adjustment of children via their drawing (cf. Machover, 1949). Her approach is primarily clinical but lacks an integrating theory.

The depiction of emotionally significant topics

The work of Machover and Koppitz (described above) was primarily aimed at personality assessment and the diagnosis of emotional disturbance. Nevertheless, there are a number of implicit assumptions in this work which relate to the depiction of emotionally significant aspects of the topic of drawing. One such assumption is that, in making a drawing, children will emphasize those elements of special interest and personal importance. Thus Machover (1949) suggested that psychosexually immature adolescent males would emphasize the breasts in their drawings of a female figure to reflect their preoccupation with that part of the body.

The idea that personally or emotionally significant items will be emphasized in a drawing is not confined to clinical analyses of art. According to some artistic conventions (for example, in the tomb paintings of Ancient Egypt) the size of a figure in a picture was sometimes used to signal the importance of the person depicted. Several authorities have claimed that children, particularly those aged six years or younger, also may use size in their drawings to signify the importance of topic.

Children of six years and younger, according to the traditional classification of drawing development introduced by Luquet (1927), do not generally achieve visually correct size scaling in their drawings. Indeed, it is easy to find examples of gross inaccuracies in scaling in drawings (see, for example, the relative sizes of the house, man and door in Figure 11.b). Observations such as this have led some authorities to conclude that for such young artists size more often reflects importance than an attempt at visually correct scaling. Thus, the man in Figure 11.b was drawn relatively too large compared to both the house and the door because, it is claimed, for the child the man was more important than the other two items.

Lowenfeld has been one of the most influential proponents of the view that children use size to signal importance in their drawing. To illustrate this effect he cites a child's drawing of a girl picking flowers (Lowenfeld and Brittain, 1975, p. 188). In this picture, the hands are exaggerated in size, reflecting (Lowenfeld claimed) their particular importance for the activity. It can also be argued that the overestimation of the size of the head relative to the body commonly found in children's human figure drawing is partly a consequence of the greater importance children attach to the head (see Freeman, 1980).

A number of studies have attempted to investigate the effects of importance of topic on size of drawing in a more systematic way. Solley and Haigh (1957), Craddick (1961) and Sechrest and Wallace (1964) have all carried out studies based on the assumption that Santa Claus increases in importance for North American children as Christmas approaches. In accordance with the importance hypothesis, Santa Claus drawings made by such children were found to increase in size the nearer to Christmas they were drawn and to decrease in size again afterwards. Interpretation of many of these findings is problematic for a number of reasons. First, in few instances have presumed differences in importance been adequately validated independently of the size differences they are purported to explain. Second, none of the studies of importance effects on drawing has taken into account the possible confounding effects on size of the amount of detail drawn on the figures. If children make their drawings of important topics more detailed than those of other topics, then larger drawings of important topics may be a consequence only of the inclusion (or the anticipated inclusion) of extra detail (Freeman, 1980). As noted in Chapter 5, a recent study by Henderson and Thomas has confirmed that children tend to enlarge the outline of figures when they intend to include additional detail within the outline.

Such an effect could conceivably explain why Santa Claus drawings get larger as Christmas approaches. Specifically, it is reasonable to suppose that children receive increasing exposure to pictures of Santa Claus over the period before Christmas. Such exposure may introduce more detail into children's drawings of Santa Claus, which then have to be made larger in order to accommodate this additional detail. The finding by Wallach and Leggett (1972) that drawings of Santa Claus do not reliably decrease in size after Christmas (when his importance is presumably on the wane) provides some support for this suggestion.

Yet another confounding factor applies when the items to be compared in size are drawn on the same sheet of paper. Specifically, there may appear to be an effect of importance on size if the more important item is drawn first and, because of inadequate planning, there is insufficient space left on the paper for a visually correct depiction of the second item. Thomas and Tsalimi (1988) have shown that such failures of planning are a factor in this usual overestimation of the size of the head when the head is drawn before the rest of the body in children's human figure drawing.

There is an additional measurement problem with studies which have looked at drawings of persons of differing importance. In many cases the more important of the persons concerned (e.g. Santa Claus, King, Queen) is associated with special headgear; and it is not easy to discover whether or not children take such headgear into account in considering the relative size of the figures.

Given these problems of interpretation it is not surprising that some authors (Freeman, 1980; Allik and Laak, 1985) have been doubtful about the existence of a general effect of importance on size in children's drawing. Recent unpublished research by Tania Fox, however, has included controls for the confounding factors and measurement problems described above, and found evidence for such an effect. In one such study, Tania Fox found that children make larger drawings of their parents than of "ordinary" men and women, even when there is no difference in the average amount of detail included in the figures. Given that we should expect parents and ordinary people to be the same average real size, this result seems to be clear evidence of an effect of significance of the topic to the drawer on the size of the drawing.

In a further study, Thomas, Chaigne and Fox (in press) asked children to copy the outline of a human figure. Children made smaller drawings of an outline characterized as a nasty person than one for which no characterization was given (Figure 22). Again, the observed differences in size could not be explained in terms of planning problems or of the amount of detail included in the drawings. This result for the nasty outline is consistent with earlier findings by Fox and Thomas (in press) that children who were scared of Halloween witches made relatively smaller drawings of witches than did children who were not scared of witches (see also Craddick, 1963). It seems, then, that drawings of threatening topics may be reduced in size. Clearly, significance *per se* is not the crucial factor: the emotions associated with the topic seem to be involved as well. It is tempting to speculate that attractive and interesting topics will be drawn larger than topics of the same real size but lacking in personal interest for the drawer; and that unattractive or threatening topics may be drawn smaller than same-sized but emotionally neutral topics.

At present there is no accepted theoretical account of how the significance of a topic is translated into the size of a child's drawing of that topic. We have already noted the possibility that this use of size may be an acquired artistic convention (big equals good or important, small equals bad or insignificant). Another possibility is that these significance effects on size are components of appetitive/defensive reactions. Thus, for example, the nasty man may have been drawn smaller to increase the psychological distance between the drawer and the topic or to minimize the threat.

It is important to note in this context that recent research of our own (Silk, 1986; Silk and Thomas, 1986, 1988) has indicated that even very young children are better at reproducing visually correct size scaling in their drawings than many authorities have previously suggested (see Chapter 6). As we have already noted (and see also Chapter 5), there are many other factors related to the process of constructing a drawing that may influence its size (planning problems, inclusion of detail). Although importance of topic can affect the size of a drawing, it would not be at all safe to assume that the size of a spontaneous free drawing in itself necessarily tells us anything about the significance of the topic for the drawer without first considering the likely contribution of these other factors to the size of the drawing.

Art therapy

Art therapy, as it is usually conducted, is based on the assumption that the expression of emotion in art has therapeutic benefits. In art therapy, the patient is encouraged to make drawings (or paintings, models, sculpture and so forth) in the presence of the therapist, who will encourage or guide the child in his/her artwork. Sometimes the child will be invited to draw whatever s/he pleases, at other times the therapist may make quite specific requests, such as "Draw your family". Without exception, art therapists assert that art therapy is suitable for all kinds of patients, not just those with some artistic ability. The underlying rationale for most forms of art therapy is that the expression of feelings and ideas in drawings has a therapeutic effect, although we may reasonably assume that drawings made in art therapy are influenced by the therapist's input as well as the child's.

Even a cursory survey of the published literature (e.g. Dalley, 1984) reveals that art therapy can take many forms. Most forms of art therapy are closely associated with one or another of the many varieties of psychodynamically-oriented psychotherapies. The rationale, aims and conduct of any particular art therapy are normally determined by the form of psychodynamic theory with which it is associated. There are, however, four aims which are common to many forms of art therapy. These aims are catharsis, insight/integration, communication and mastery.

Catharsis is the idea in Freudian psychoanalytic theory that the confrontation and expression of blocked and suppressed feelings is therapeutic. Thus, for example, a child who expresses her envy of and repressed hostility towards her younger brother in an appropriate drawing will thereby gain some relief from the conflicts and tension generated by these feelings (see also Chapter 4).

Insight and integration is often claimed to be an important consequence of engaging in art. Dalley (1984, p. xiii) suggests that art therapy is "a way of stating mixed, poorly understood feelings in an attempt to bring them into clarity and order." For children, who may often lack verbal labels for many of their feelings, expression in images may be particularly useful.

Communication in art therapy means communication between the child and the therapist. Pictorial communication, it is claimed, can have special advantages in situations where the child is unable or unwilling to talk about her/his experiences and feelings. It has been noted that communication problems may often arise when children have suffered some kind of physical (perhaps sexual) abuse. They may be shy about talking about normally taboo subjects, they may lack comprehension or appropriate words to describe their experiences or they may fear retribution from an abuser who may have demanded secrecy. Children thus inhibited from talking may find it easier to communicate their experiences in drawings (see, for example, Goodwin, 1982).

Mastery refers to the suggestion that by recreating difficult situations in drawings, children can gain some experience of mastery over their problems. In recreating the situation the child thus also acquires some control over her/his own feelings and reactions. Piaget's concept of assimilation through play is one expression of this idea – the notion of striving for control which is important in later developments of psychoanalytic theory is another. Erikson (1968), for example, stressed the value of restoring a sense of mastery by recreating difficult episodes in pretend play, stories or drawing.

Much of the support claimed for art therapy is in the form of successful case histories and the clinical judgement of experienced practitioners. For adult patients there are many case studies that suggest that involvement in art is accompanied by improvement in the patient (for a review, see Winner, 1982). In the case of schizophrenic adult patients, for example, their paintings often reflect the course of their illness. Paintings by severely disturbed patients often comprise a mass of unintegrated detail; when the patient starts to recover, the paintings become less bizarre and more structured. We do not know, however, whether the artwork assisted the recovery or merely reflected it.

As far as we are aware, there are no published reports of controlled evaluations of art therapy with children. We would expect, however, that the effectiveness of art therapy will be subject to the same factors known to influence the effectiveness of psychotherapy with which art therapy is closely linked. The principal factors determining the effectiveness of psychotherapy seem to be the personal qualities of the therapist and his/her empathy with the patient (Truax and Carkhuff, 1967). This conclusion has been confirmed repeatedly (see Bergin, 1975). Some patients in psychotherapy become markedly better, but some become dramatically worse. A similar picture has emerged from surveys of encounter groups which are often a form of group psychotherapy. Although the main factor determining the outcome of treatment seems to be the style of the group leader or therapist, different forms of psychotherapy have also been found to differ in their efficacy (Smith and Glass, 1977). To the extent that art therapy and psychotherapy are similar endeavours sharing aims and rationale in common, then we might expect similar variations in the effectiveness of art therapy, depending on the procedures used and the characteristics of the therapist. What we need now are properly controlled outcome studies in which patients in art therapy are compared with similar patients receiving an alternative form of treatment.

Summary

Children's drawings have often been interpreted in clinical tests of personality and emotional adjustment. There are some features that are more frequent in the drawings made by emotionally disturbed children than in those made by normal children. There is, however, little empirical support for many of the specific personality interpretations often placed on children's drawing. Recent research has begun to identify some general principles governing children's depictions of personally significant topics, which are often drawn larger than neutral or unimportant topics. There is also some evidence that threatening topics may be drawn smaller than neutral ones. Art therapy is based on the assumption that the expression of emotion in art is therapeutic, but we know of no well-controlled studies to evaluate this suggestion.

8 Exceptional drawing development

So far in this book we have focused our attention on the typical drawing development of normal children. We now turn to consider some cases of exceptional drawing ability. To set such ability into an appropriate context we must first examine briefly the usual course of drawing development beyond childhood.

By the time children reach puberty, we find that, for many, drawing is no longer a natural activity (Koppitz, 1984). For some children, many of their drawings produced at this age are of a poorer quality compared to those made a few years earlier. Little effort seems to be made in drawing and more often now quick and carelessly drawn, stereotyped figures and cartoons emerge copied from the images seen on television and in comic books. For other children drawing generally seems no longer to be attractive and they simply refuse to draw at all. A possible explanation, suggested by Kellogg (1970), is that children may come to regard drawing as a childish and immature form of self-expression and feel some social pressure not to engage in it, at least not in public (see also Arnheim, 1969). A related factor, noted by Gardner (1980), is that many children in early adolescence become very self-conscious and self-critical:

The youth can more rigorously criticize her own works and the works of others. Naturally this heightened ability exerts a crucial influence on her own artistic output; for if at such a time of critical scrupulousness one's own artistry is found wanting, the pressures to cease may prove irresistible. (Gardner, 1980, p. 213)

Koppitz suggests that such children may turn instead to language, sports or music in order to express their feelings.

According to Koppitz (1984), however, there are at least four groups of youngsters who do continue to produce drawings when they get older. These are first, artistically gifted or talented youngsters; second, language-impaired adolescents; third, immature adolescents; and fourth, emotionally disturbed youngsters. Many of these children, according to Koppitz, will continue to produce drawings long after most other children of their age have lost interest in this activity.

In this chapter we shall concentrate on children who exhibit unusual ability in their drawing. We shall consider artistically-gifted but otherwise normal children; and a small but special group of autistic children who show a special talent for drawing. The autistic children have increasingly intrigued art critics and psychologists over the last decade or so. What is so unusual about these children is that, despite being severely mentally handicapped, they are able to produce stunningly realistic drawings, thereby far surpassing the drawing abilities of normal children of a similar chronological age.

The development of drawing talent in otherwise normal children

The history of art indicates that many professional artists exhibited a special talent for drawing in their childhood. Park (1978), for example, found eighteen child prodigies in fourteenth- to sixteenth-century Italy in Vasari's *Lives of the Most Eminent Painters* (1912–1914). These Renaissance children were, apparently, producing work of professional adult standard by the age of eight or nine years. More recent examples, such as the childhood artwork of Picasso and Klee, undoubtedly indicate exceptional draughtsmanship at an early age (Gardner, 1980). Nevertheless, there is nothing corresponding to Mozart's musical achievements at the age of four years. In the visual arts, it seems, aesthetically significant work, by adult standards, does not usually emerge until adolescence, even for great artists such as Picasso (see Gardner, 1973).

Winner (1982) has suggested that there are major similar-ities between the drawing development of normal and gifted children, although there are also some interesting differences. According to Winner (and to Gardner, 1980), gifted children progress through the same sequence of drawing development as do normal children, but do so more quickly. An important source of evidence described by both Winner and Gardner was an exhibition organized by Ayala Gordon at the Israel Museum in Jerusalem (1979). This exhibition contained examples of the adult and childhood work of a number of well-known Israeli artists. The drawings of these gifted individuals could then be compared with drawings made by normal (non-gifted) children of the same age.

According to Winner (1982), both normal and gifted children passed through a pre-conventional stage in which drawings were simple, expressive and apparently well composed (at least to adult eyes). At this (pre-school) level, the gifted children drew more naturalistically (using fluid contours) than did the normal children, who were more likely to construct their drawings out of simple shapes (see Chapter 5 and Figure 10). At some point after the age of six years, both normal and gifted children appeared to progress eventually to a conventional style of drawing, the gifted children doing so at an earlier age than the normal children. Winner described the drawings at this stage as less aesthetically pleasing to adults than earlier drawings in terms of both fluidity of line and balance of their composition. Instead, the drawings displayed a concern for the accurate depiction of detail and the use of conventionalized schemata. For many of the normal children this conventional stage marked the limit of their drawing development. In contrast, the drawing of the gifted children continued to evolve and by early adolescence many had acquired a distinctive personal style. Thus the drawing of gifted children seemed to develop in the same way as that of normal children, but did so at a faster rate and progressed further (see also Lark-Horovitz, Lewis and Luca, 1967).

A more detailed account of talented drawing development, and the conditions which encourage it, has been provided by Gardner (1980) in the form of case histories of two talented youngsters. Gardner argued that for adolescents to develop their talent, they had to overcome the self-consciousness and self-criticism typical of their age group. They had to come to feel, instead, that they accomplished something worthwhile in their drawing. Such a sense of accomplishment, he suggested, depended in turn on the ready availability of opportunities to practise drawing and an appreciation of the child's efforts by others.

Some art educators (e.g. Lowenfeld, 1947) have claimed that teaching in art should be essentially non-directive and concerned mainly with the provision of materials and encouragement. Gardner, however, was doubtful about the prospects for the development of talent by self-education alone and considered that some degree of formal training in art should be provided, in order to enlarge the child's repertoire of techniques and increase artistic awareness (see also Wilson and Wilson, 1977). Like Lowenfeld, however, Gardner (1980) also acknowledged the importance of preserving some degree of individuality and originality in drawing. Only that way, he claimed, will such talented adolescents keep communicating in their drawings.

Gardner's case histories of talented youngsters allowed him to identify several characteristics of drawing development in adolescence. According to Gardner (1980), the need to conform and make purely realistic pictures progressively wanes as the youngsters develop a personal style of drawing and become more artistically ambitious as time goes on. Gardner noted also that adolescents draw not only what makes sense to them in a personal way, but also draw imaginary objects and people. Thoughts and emotions may now be consciously expressed in drawings which are highly personal and individual. As in much modern art, colours no longer have to correspond to those in the real world. Instead, the artists are concerned with evoking a mood or a certain emotion either in themselves or in others who look at their drawings.

To summarize, we can see that otherwise normal children who develop their drawing talent do so by following the same pattern of drawing development as most other children. They differ in showing greater skill and in continuing to practise and improve their drawing into adolescence. For many such children, their art becomes more personal and expressive in ways that are similar to much contemporary art produced by professional artists.

The gifted autistic artist

In the previous chapters of this book we have outlined and explained the course of normal drawing development in young children. Whereas talented children seem to progress through these stages of drawing development more quickly than do normal children, the course of their development is essentially similar. There are, however, a very few children who also show superb artistry in their drawings, but who may have achieved this level of skill via a different route. What makes these drawings even more unusual is the fact that the children who made them have usually been diagnosed as autistic or mentally retarded.

In 1943, Leo Kanner described a small group of mentally retarded children who had strikingly failed to develop normal social relationships. Kanner (1943) proposed the term "infantile autism" to describe this disorder. Other characteristics of the disorder include impaired language development and (frequently) an obsessive desire for stability, order and sameness in their environment. Indeed, such children sometimes appear to regard even their own parents as objects and to live in their own private world, far out of reach of any human contact.

In the past the diagnosis of infantile autism has been problematic. In North America, autism did not appear as a diagnostic category in DSM-I (1952) or in DSM-II (1968), but it has finally been included in DSM-III (1980). The diagnostic criteria specified in DSM-III include the symptoms outlined above and specify onset before the age of thirty months. In contrast, Wing (1976), working in England, has argued that "early childhood autism" is a more appropriate term for the disorder, because in some cases the condition does not become apparent until the second or third year of life.

Although the cause of infantile autism still has not been firmly established, we now have detailed descriptions of the disorder and its prognosis. Davison and Neale (1982) noted that somewhere between two to four cases per 10,000 children have been diagnosed with this condition. Although most autistic children score in the mentally retarded range on IQ tests, some of these children display extraordinary talents in certain very isolated areas, often in music or mathematical calculations (see Howe and Smith, 1988, and Treffert, 1989). According to Gardner (1980), such "islands of skill" are symptomatic and even diagnostic of autism. The exceptional skills of these so-called *idiots savants* were often achieved in their adulthood and involved unusual abilities of memory. Our present discussion concerns a very few autistic individuals who have displayed quite extraordinary ability in making viewer-centred drawings.

Exceptional drawing ability in autistic artists: some case studies

Nadia is probably the most well-known and most thoroughly investigated case of exceptional drawing ability in an autistic child. As reported by Selfe (1977), Nadia displayed several characteristic features of autism (social isolation, retarded language development) at an early age. Nadia's mother reported that Nadia began to draw at the age of three, and that even her early drawings displayed evidence of exceptional skill. Although Nadia clearly suffered large cognitive and emotional deficits, she drew animals, and especially horses, with amazing accuracy and manual dexterity, apparently skipping all usual drawing stages, such as those of scribbling and tadpoles.

According to Selfe (1977), Nadia would often study a picture for weeks before attempting to draw that same picture herself. She did not copy the pictures directly, but appeared to draw from memory. A similar form of delayed performance (see Park, 1978) has also been found in other autistic children who show outstanding recall of phrases or melodies long after their first presentation.

In the process of making her drawings, Nadia was like a sophisticated adult artist, drawing bits and pieces all over the page, eventually combining them all with a few quick and strongly drawn strokes, thereby showing superb mastery of realism. Tests in other areas suggested that Nadia had eidetic memory; that is, she was capable of seeing distinctly in her mind's eye scenes she had previously seen in the real world around her (Selfe, 1977). However, it has been found that a small but significant percentage of all elementary school children have eidetic memory (Haber, 1979). Consequently, this ability alone could not account for Nadia's unbelievable drawings. In addition, she would frequently use a new orientation and add or omit certain details, sometimes even varying the sizes of the objects, thus displaying a flexibility in depiction which eidetic memory alone could not account for.

From the age of about four years, Nadia's drawings displayed mastery of perspective and foreshortening in detailed and viewer-centred drawings which an accomplished adolescent artist would find hard to match. She was able to draw three-dimensonial objects on two-dimensional paper from an early age, and by the age of six years her sense of proportion was well developed (see Chapter 6).

Another example of autistic talent is provided by the artwork of Yamamoto in Japan. As reported by Morishima (1974), Yamamoto was very severely retarded with a reported maximum tested IQ of 47. In his childhood this boy copied stereotyped cartoons, but in contrast to his human figure drawings which were very poor, his drawings of buildings showed very good accuracy. In contrast to Nadia, who was essentially self-taught, Yamamoto was given formal training in drawing to encourage and develop his artistic talent. As the result of this long-term educational programme, Yamamoto became a successful professional artist. *A propos* the present interest, it is a pity that this boy's skills were not noticed until he was about thirteen years old, and so we lack information on his early drawing development.

Yet another case of anomalous drawing ability has been described by Sacks (1985). This case is somewhat different from those of Nadia and Yamamoto in that it concerns the drawings of a twenty-one-year-old man, José, who had been diagnosed with secondary autism, resulting from brain disease in late childhood. Like Nadia, however, José was able to draw very quickly and accurately, paying attention to minute details of the picture or objects shown to him.

In his interpretation of José's drawings, Sacks suggested that José saw the world around him as forms, which he first experienced and absorbed, and which he then reproduced. Sacks was firmly of the opinion that José was not only capable of visually realistic drawings, but that he could also make his drawings funny or to some extent expressive (see Chapter 9).

A slightly more complicated case is that of Stephen Wiltshire (1987), whose incredible drawings have been published since he appeared on television. When his book of drawings was published, Stephen was a twelve-year-old autistic child with an amazing sense of detail, especially for buildings, his favourite drawing subject. According to Casson (in Wiltshire, 1987), Stephen's drawings were often based on an initial observation of a building. He seemed to stand and watch the building rather than observe it and would later draw a detailed and viewer-centred drawing of that building from memory. Stephen's passion for buildings and their details is evident in his drawing of Westminster Abbey reproduced as Figure 23 in this book.

Comparisons with other populations

In seeking explanations for the drawing skills of autistic artists, most investigators have implicitly or explicitly compared them to other autistic children or to normal children. Of course, such comparisons are hard to make with any confidence because of the very small numbers of exceptional autistic artists who have been found and studied.

Comparisons with other autistic children reveal few systematic differences between autistic artists and other autistic children. It seems that the only clear characteristic which distinguishes autistic artists from other autistic children is their exceptional drawing skill itself (but see discussion below of O'Connor and Hermelin, 1987b). Autistic artists share with other autistic children their lack of language development, social isolation and an obsession with regularity and sameness. It has been suggested (e.g. Selfe, 1977) that eidetic memory may play a role in the exceptional drawing talent of some autistic artists such as Nadia. Interestingly, the exceptional musical and mathematical feats of some other *idiots savants* may also depend on exceptional memory. We should note, however, that significant numbers of normal as well as handicapped children appear to have eidetic memory and that there is no known correlation between possession of eidetic memory and other cognitive or intellectual abilities (Haber, 1979). We know of no systematically collected evidence that otherwise normal children with eidetic memory have exceptional drawing talent.

In comparison with the drawings of normal children, the work of autistic artists is strikingly different in several respects. First, the graphic skill of autistic artists is not only superior to their general (retarded) level of intellectual functioning, but also quite superior to the drawing achieved by normal children at a comparable chronological age. Second, none of the autistic children reported had any interest at all in portraying colour in their pictures. Nadia, for example, did not include colours spontaneously, not even when the original pictures from which her drawings were derived were themselves highly coloured. In general, autistic artists do not appear to want to use colour even as a further means to make their pictures more visually realistic. However, perhaps we should not be too surprised that autistic artists show little interest in colour because they do not seem to be concerned to depict feelings and moods on paper, for which colour is often used by normal talented youngsters (Gardner, 1980).

In contrast, young normal children readily employ colour in their drawings and have favourite colours. Lowenfeld (1947), however, considers that a conventional use of colour (grass is green, sky is blue) may not appear in normal children's drawings until the age of eight years.

Third, and related to the previous point, autistic artists seem to have different preferred drawing topics from normal children. As noted earlier (Chapter 2), the human figure is the preferred drawing topic for most normal children. In contrast, autistic artists seem to have had what can best be described as an obsessional interest in a few special topics, rarely including the human figure. (Stephen and Yamamoto were interested in buildings, Nadia was interested in horses and cockerels.)

Fourth, while young normal children mainly make schematic and symbolic representations, the autistic artists described above were accomplished at making highly detailed and viewer-centred pictures, often from an early age. Selfe (1983) has noted several types of view-specific information, such as reduction in size with distance, occlusion and foreshortening, which autistic artists have often included in their drawings, but which are infrequent in the drawings of normal children of a comparable age.

Finally, it has been reported (e.g. Park, 1978) that, generally, none of the autistic children reviewed so far seems to take much pleasure in praise given for their drawings, or indeed shows any sense of pleasure in displaying their drawings. However, we believe that Stephen Wiltshire may be a possible exception to this generalization. Not only do his drawings seem to be made in a possibly more meticulous and more organized way than those of other autistic artists, but he also showed interest in his own drawing performance on television and commented on how glad he was that other people liked his drawings. Perhaps this greater interest, together with his self-critical awareness, is what makes Stephen, at least for the moment, continue his drawing with great enthusiasm.

Explanations of drawing ability in autistic artists

A widely-held view of artistic talent in autistic children is that it is partly a product of such children's language difficulties (see, for example, Arnheim, 1980; Paine, 1981; Selfe, 1977, 1983). Specifically, Selfe (1977) has suggested that Nadia did not draw well in spite of her mental handicaps but because of them. A further five children with exceptional drawing ability studied by Selfe (1983) also displayed language deficits, which led her to conclude that the lack of language development in these children played a major part in their drawings.

To appreciate how the lack of language development could facilitate drawing, we need to take account of some current ideas about the cognitive abilities necessary for the production of visually realistic drawings. As we have noted earlier (Chapter 5), knowing the structure of an object is not sufficient for a child to be able to make an accurate view-specific picture of that object. What seems to be required in addition is a graphic description or drawing schema (Phillips *et al.*, 1985). There are some reasons for believing that ability to deploy graphic descriptions is independent of intelligence (O'Connor and Hermelin, 1987a) and thus that general mental retardation need not prevent the development of exceptional drawing skill. Paivio's dual-coding theory (Paivio, 1971) suggests that there are two distinct forms of internal representations which may be employed in thinking – verbal and imaginal. Applying this distinction to drawing development, Selfe proposed that, for normal children, the often dominant influence of the verbal mode results in drawings that are symbolic in the sense in which language is symbolic. Verbal proficiency contributes to normal children's ability to abstract, generalize and symbolize. A consequence of language development and the influence of verbal coding produces one of the most distinctive features of normal drawing development – namely, that before the age of eight years (approximately) visual realism is seldom the normal child's prime concern.

In many cases, young normal children "draw what they know, not what they see", or they produce schematic drawings that symbolize the topic depicted rather than convey its precise appearance. In essence, Selfe's theory implies that normal children's development of language and conceptual knowledge of objects interferes with optical realism. Freeman and Janikoun (1972), for example, have demonstrated that children will often draw an object in its canonical orientation, regardless of the position in which that object has been presented to them (see Chapter 6). These arguments put the schematic and symbolic drawings of normal children in a new light, showing how advanced children's thinking must be in order to portray their conceptual understanding. The making of a schematic caricature involves the identification of important and defining features of an object, a selection of attributes that is not required in the production of a detailed, viewer-centred drawing.

Selfe (1983) then suggested that the underdevelopment of verbal coding in autistic children allows imaginal coding to dominate their thinking and more especially their drawing. It has been found that mentally handicapped people with exceptional drawing talent are superior to IQ-matched control subjects in their ability to identify incomplete pictures (O'Connor and Hermelin, 1987b), which suggests superior use of visual imagery. It has been suggested that the autistic artists seem never to go through a stage in their drawing development in which they are not concerned with viewer-centred representations. As far as we can tell, at an age when normal children produce symbolic and schematic drawings, autistic artists typically produce static, spatial and viewer-centred pictures. We do not know for certain whether or not the drawing stages which normal children go through in their drawing development are completely absent in the development of gifted autistic children. Nadia, for example, seemed to skip the various scribbling, schematic and tadpole stages. Instead, her works "exhibited skill with perspective, foreshortening, and other tricks of the artist's trade, ones usually acquired only after years of patient drill and evolution of the 'natural' drawing capacity" (Gardner, 1980, p. 182). However, it remains a possibility, as Gardner and other authors have commented, that Nadia went through the normal drawing stages before the age at which she was first studied, and in a matter of a few days.

Nevertheless, the production of viewer-centred drawings could be a consequence of an inability to abstract and symbolize. If correct, this hypothesis implies that the only option open for autistic artists is to draw precisely what they see. However, a lack of symbolizing ability is, presumably, a handicap shared by all autistic children, only a few of whom are gifted artists. It seems only reasonable, therefore, to conclude that there must be an additional factor which makes some autistic children so talented at drawing. Could it be that excellent visual memory alone is not enough and that an ability to encode it into motor hand movement is needed?

Furthermore, as Selfe (1983) has pointed out, the drawings of artistic autistic children *are* symbolic to the extent that they are two-dimensional representations of objects in three-dimensional space. What autistic children often cannot recognize, however, is how these objects they draw are members of certain categories. Selfe (1977), for example, noted that although Nadia could visually remember all the aspects of an object, she could not categorize that object on the basis of its function (she could not categorize two types of chair).

It is possible that in some autistic artists, whose speech development is often very retarded, other associative processes develop at a quicker rate (O'Connor and Hermelin, 1987a). Such compensatory development could be similar to, for example, someone who is blind and who has developed a much stronger awareness of smell and sound compared to a sighted person.

In support of the notion that verbal coding interferes with the development of viewer-centred representations, Selfe (1977, 1983) has noted that Nadia, since her speech has started to develop, has produced fewer and less skilful drawings. Unlike

Nadia, however, Stephen Wiltshire's drawing has been seemingly unaffected although his language has developed enormously from the age of about five onward. What is more, as Stephen is getting older he is becoming more aware and self-critical of his drawings, setting himself higher standards all the time. In contrast to Nadia then, who gradually drew less and less, Stephen has not only learnt to talk, read and write, even though sometimes with difficulty, but at the same time has managed to keep his extraordinary vision and graphic talent. It may not be inevitable, therefore, that development of language will displace exceptional talent for drawing in autistic artists.

Although the autistic children with anomalous graphic abilities make drawings which are viewer-centred and which show a very accurate sense of perspective, they usually show no more than that. Unlike the drawings of talented normal youngsters (see above) the artwork of autistic children seldom conveys anything more than a visual appearance. There is seldom, for example, any expression of emotion or of personal relationships (but see Sacks, 1985). Such a lack of emotional expression is, of course, consistent with the topics which many autistic artists choose to draw - buildings rather than people.

Summary

Many children gradually stop drawing as they get older, but there are some children who develop their talent further once they have reached adolescence. These young, talented but otherwise normal artists show a similar pattern of drawing development to that found in other normal children, but progress further and at a faster rate. Exceptional talent at drawing is also occasionally found in severely handicapped autistic children. These autistic artists characteristically produce viewer-centred drawings at an age when normal children produce schematic caricatures. Why some autistic children show this exceptional drawing ability is still not known with certainty. One possibility is that their talent for visually realistic pictures is related to their lack of verbal development and an associated inability to categorize objects and to abstract their defining features.

9 Children's drawings as art

In earlier chapters we have seen how a child's drawing can convey information about the structure and appearance of its topic and how the significance of the topic may affect a drawing. We have also seen that the procedures children use to construct their drawings can also influence the final form of a drawing. But to suggest that a child's drawings can also be considered as art introduces a totally new dimension – that of their aesthetic and expressive qualities.

We cannot begin to discuss this issue until we have a definition of art that will allow us to specify what the artistic properties of a drawing are. As you might expect, it is not easy to supply a definition of art that covers all the great variety of artistic works, ranging from poetry, music and dance to painting and drawing, and yet excludes items that most people would not consider as art. Defining art simply as self-expression, for example, would lead us to include grunts, groans and screams as art. On the other hand, limiting art to products of human skill would exclude discovered art (see Blank, Massey, Gardner and Winner, 1984, for further discussion of this problem).

In an attempt to resolve the problems of defining art, Goodman (1968) has suggested that, although precise criteria cannot be established, there are some identifiable properties that works of art tend to possess, and that are generally not possessed by other things. These include repleteness, expression and composition.

Repleteness refers to the way in which more aspects of an object become significant when it is viewed as a work of art than when it is not treated as art. Repleteness of a drawing as a work of art, for example, refers to the way in which variations in the thickness, density and smoothness of a line, in addition to the thing it represents, can all contribute to its artistic impact.

Expression (or metaphorical exemplification) in a work of art refers to the extent to which it conveys feelings, moods or ideas.

A drawing of a person who looks sad represents the emotion of sadness but need not express sadness; such an expression may instead be conveyed by the use of certain colors (often dark), properties of line (drooping), and the like. (Carothers and Gardner, 1979, p. 571)

Composition of a work of art, such as a drawing, refers to the way in which the drawing has a structure, so that, for example, the two halves of the picture are in visual balance (see Arnheim, 1956). Of course, many things which are not works of art have balanced structures, but structure or composition is particularly important in works of art.

It follows from Goodman's characterization of art that all works of art should be expressive of something. Goodman (1968) has argued that even apparently non-representational works of art are symbolic and have expressive properties. Such works of art could be said to be symbolic of ideas or emotions. The principal opposing view - that some artworks are aesthetically pleasing in themselves regardless of reference - has a long history. A modern exponent is Monroe Beardsley (1958, 1979). The question of whether or not an object must refer to something else to be considered as art is, however, not immediately relevant to our present interest. It is perhaps worth noting that some of the power of great works of art seems to derive from their reference to other matters (see, for example, Picasso's painting "Guernica"). These questions are discussed at greater length by Dickie (1985) and by Blank *et al.* (1984).

Eisner (1972) has suggested that children's artistic capacities be considered as falling into three areas: their ability to produce drawings having expressive and aesthetic properties; their ability to perceive these properties in the work of others; and their understanding of art as a cultural phenomenon. In each of these three areas - production, perception and understanding - we shall consider whether or not children are sensitive to the three properties of art identified by Goodman - repleteness, expression and composition.

Can children produce drawings with artistic properties?

To be considered as art a child's drawing must have both expressive and aesthetic qualities. One kind of expressive drawing (discussed in Chapter 7) is that which contains emotional indicators as defined by Koppitz (1968). Should such drawings by emotionally disturbed children be considered as art because they express emotion? According to Goodman's definition, such a drawing would have to display repleteness and good composition as well as express emotion to count as art. Our own judgement, having looked at collections of the drawings made by emotionally disturbed children (Koppitz, 1968; Schildkrout *et al.*, 1972), is that some, but not necessarily all, drawings containing emotional indicators could be considered as art. The occurrence of a clinically reliable emotional indicator on its own is not sufficient to qualify a drawing as art.

In contrast, the typical drawings made by normal (non-disturbed) children have been considered as art by many influential artists and authorities on art; that is to say, they regard these drawings as aesthetically pleasing (showing repleteness and composition) and expressive. The main basis for these claims is that there are similarities between typical examples of children's drawing and some styles of primitive art and modern art. We shall explore each of these comparisons in turn.

A comparison with modern art

There can be no doubting the widespread appeal that very young children's drawings (and paintings) currently holds for many adults in Western societies. Many experts (e.g. Arnheim, 1956; Lowenfeld and Brittain, 1975; Gardner, 1980) have commented on the resemblances between the drawings (and paintings) of very young children and those of famous artists such as Klee, Klimt, Miro and Picasso, to name but a few. The resemblance is no accident. The professional artists have consciously copied the style of young children's drawing. Klee in particular studied and was influenced by children's art in the same way that Picasso and Modigliani sought inspiration from African sculpture and carving (Efland, 1976).

So close, indeed, is the similarity between children's drawings and some examples of modern art that it is possible to intermingle drawings and paintings made by children with those of professional artists and fool even art students as to the identities of the creators (see Ecker, 1976). To date, most of the artistic interest in children's drawing has centred on the work of children under the age of eight or nine years: the drawings of most older children have generally been thought to be of less merit artistically, which is probably the reason why no professional artists have attempted to copy their style.

We should also note that it is only in the present century that there are any similarities at all between child and adult art. No one is ever likely to confuse the art of Rembrandt, or even Cézanne, with the work of young children. This point reminds us that adults' artistic judgements and ideals are not based entirely on absolute standards of what is beautiful, but reflect acquired tastes, conditioned by culture and experience. More specifically, recent empirical research suggests that the most significant influence on each successive revolution in artistic style and taste is the art that preceded it (see Martindale, 1984). In other words, our current ideas of what is artistically pleasing are, in part, a reaction to earlier fashions in artistic taste. Indeed, in choosing children's style of drawing and painting as a source of inspiration, modern artists were quite deliberately reacting against pre-existing standards of artistic taste. Miro and Picasso, for example, were intentionally analytic and destructive of conventional representational techniques in their painting, although both could and did produce highly realistic perspective pictures when they wanted to. *A propos* the present interest, prior to the nineteenth century (when realistic depiction was the accepted ideal) it is doubtful that anyone ever considered for one moment that there was any artistic merit in young children's drawing. If Martindale is correct, we should also expect that future generations may not find young children's drawing quite as artistically interesting as we do now.

The current widespread acceptance of children's work as art can be traced back to the influence of such authorities as Franz Cizek in Vienna. In 1897 Cizek founded an art class whose guiding principles have remained influential up to the present time. It is largely to Cizek that we owe the widely-held doctrine that young children have a natural aptitude for art. It is interesting to note that Cizek himself was apparently interested in children's art only for its artistic qualities. He was not concerned, as was Lowenfeld, with the possibility that there were therapeutic and general educational benefits from encouraging artistic development in children (see Efland, 1976).

We should beware, however, of reading too much into our own culturally-conditioned reactions to children's drawing and concluding, in consequence, that every child is an untaught artistic genius. The fact that we, as adults, find children's drawings artistically pleasing does not mean that children have artistic intentions and sensibilities any more than our pleasure in the shape and texture of an attractively weathered stone means that the wind and the rain have artistic ability.

It is true that young children's drawing generally follows an identifiable developmental sequence and generally has properties such as symmetry and simplicity which adults currently find appealing. The properties we find attractive, however, need have little to do with artistic considerations. Turn back to look at Figure 2.a, which shows two drawings of a human figure. The (typical) overestimation of the size of the head and the omission of arms (and other "non-essential" features) contribute to the overall simplicity of the figures and, perhaps to their artistic appeal for adults. Such drawings might well exemplify Kandinsky's claim that in the art of the child we find "a direct expression of the interior essence of things" (see Efland, 1976). Nevertheless, we have already seen (in Chapter 5) that the overestimation of the size of the head is likely to be a consequence of a failure in planning the drawing and the omission of the arms, but not the legs, a consequence of an end-anchoring effect (Freeman, 1980). Thus, the aspects of children's drawing that adults find artistically interesting may be no more than happy accidents (Winner, 1982). The features that adults find expressive, for example, may not have been drawn with any expressive intention. We discuss below the extent to which children themselves are aware of artistic properties and possibilities in drawing.

A comparison with primitive art

Several investigators have commented on the similarities between children's drawing and the adult art of other cultures. Underlying these comparisons is the assumption that certain shapes, patterns and styles of picture making have a natural and intrinsic appeal to human beings. Arnheim (1956), for example, claimed that certain visual compositions and shapes have an intrinsic appeal, or goodness of form, and that such compositions appear regularly even in the drawings that very young children produce. The same assumption of an innate artistic sense also underlies Kellogg's suggestion that there are certain patterns, such as the mandala, which have a universal appeal and recur both in children's drawing and in the art of primitive people (Kellogg, 1970). In order to evaluate such claims, we shall first consider the evidence for regarding children's drawing and primitive art to be fundamentally similar.

Kellogg (1970), as we have noted previously, collected a great many children's drawings and identified orderly progressions and developments in the appearance of certain shapes and compositions. While the many illustrations she provided often seem persuasive, it is important to remember that her analyses were not systematic and we cannot be sure how representative of children's drawings her conclusions were. The same cautions must be applied to her comments about the shapes and patterns to be found in primitive art.

A more thorough analysis of cross-cultural comparisons has been made by Deregowski in numerous publications over many years. In particular, Deregowski (1984) has noted that there are some "distortions" – that is, departures from viewer-centred perspective pictures – which can be found both in children's drawing and in the adult art of some cultures. The presentation of typical views, juxtapositions of typical views and X-ray pictures are three examples of such distortions.

We have already discussed typical views, of course, as canonical representations (see Chapter 6). Canonical representations are indeed common in the drawings of children younger than six or seven years. Deregowski (1984) notes that many examples of palaeolithic art involve the depiction of an isolated figure, often an animal, in a canonical orientation. Thus, in the cave paintings (such as the caves of Lascaux) the animals are almost always drawn in profile, human figures are drawn full face. (Deregowski describes the common preference for portraying typical views as a distortion, because typical views do not predominate in our everyday perceptual experience of the world).

Juxtapositions of typical views is another common feature of some styles of adult art. In the art of Ancient Egypt, for example, the faces of human figures were usually presented in profile, but with the eyes in front view. A similar juxtaposition of several views in the same picture is often regarded as the hallmark of American Indian art of the North-West. This kind of picture usually combines two side-views in a symmetrical composition – they are sometimes referred to as "split" figures or as "chain-type" drawings. Children also sometimes present different parts of a drawing in its canonical orientation thus achieving a similar juxtaposition of views. Deregowski (1984) compares drawings of a cat made by a young American girl and by a South Sea Islander. The two drawings are strikingly similar and both provide frontal views of the cat's head combined with typical side views of the bodies. Figures 7.b and 5.b illustrate similar compositions for children's drawings of a dog and a horse, respectively. Deregowski (1970, 1980) argued that there is a natural and universal tendency to prefer such split representations, but that this natural preference is suppressed in the drawings of older Western children, because visually realistic perspective pictures are often presented as the desired style of depiction.

What Deregowski described as X-ray drawings, we have called transparencies (see Chapters 2 and 6). We are concerned here only with that class of transparency drawing which seems to be motivated by a desire to portray normally hidden elements. Just as some children's drawings show the hidden contents of the body (see the baby in the womb in Figure 5.a), so apparently do some examples of primitive art show the skeleton in animal drawings. Deregowski (1984) presents examples of art from Canada and Australia in which a wolf and a crocodile respectively are shown with a representation of the spine running down the back.

We need to be careful not to overestimate the extent of the similarities between children's drawing and the adult art of other cultures. Systematic as opposed to selective comparisons have been rather rare. As Alland (1983) has suggested, it would place cross-cultural comparisons of this kind on a sounder footing if investigators considered the process of constructing drawings and not just the form of the finished products. With ancient art, of course, the most we can hope to do is to reconstruct something of what the sequence of making the picture may have been. There are, however, some contemporary cultures whose art is still relatively untouched by Western influences. The effort to investigate their drawing strategies and processes would surely be worthwhile. The analyses presented earlier in this book concerning the drawing process in Western children should provide some useful specific hypotheses upon which initial investigations could be based.

Granted, however, that there are some real similarities to be found between children's drawing and the adult art of other cultures, what then is the significance of these similarities for our discussion of the artistic status of children's drawing? While it seems to us that children's drawing and primitive art may have compositional properties in common, it is less clear that they share similar expressive properties. It seems to us very doubtful, for example, that children have the same artistic intentions and purposes (at least at a conscious level) as did the adult artists whose work we have been discussing. The difference between adult art and children's drawing becomes most striking when the very different functions it performs are considered. Most primitive adult art is created with a religious, magical or other social purpose in mind. It is not at all clear whether children have comparable expressive purposes in mind when they make their drawings (see Chapter 4). While we do not rule out the possibility that children's drawing has artistic properties as defined above, we do not think comparisons with primitive art provide convincing evidence at least for expressive properties. It is also worth remembering Freeman's warning that the frequent occurrence of a shape or pattern in children's drawing does not necessarily mean that children prefer that composition (Freeman, 1980).

Can children perceive artistic properties in drawing?

As we have argued above, to show that children have artistic capacities we need to do more than simply note that they often produce shapes and pictures that are similar to some examples of adult art and that adults currently find pleasing. More convincing evidence of artistic capacities in young children would be a demonstration that they respond with appropriate aesthetic judgements to their own and other people's drawings.

Until recently, most of the systematically collected evidence on this subject came from a study by Carothers and Gardner (1979). They attempted to assess children's sensitivity to two important characteristics of art – syntactic repleteness and expression (see earlier discussion of Goodman, 1968). A set of tasks was devised in which children were asked to complete drawings with distinctive features relating to repleteness and expression. They were then asked to match drawings on the basis of these properties. Five-year-old children showed little capacity either to detect or produce repleteness and expression in line drawings. Nine-year-olds were able to perceive these characteristics in drawings made by others, and twelve-year-old children showed considerable capacity to exhibit these artistic characteristics in their own drawing.

A more recent study by Itskowitz, Glaubman and Hoffman (1988), however, has suggested that Carothers and Gardner may have underestimated young children's awareness of dimensions such as line quality in their judgements of drawings. Itskowitz *et al.* tested children with nine drawings of a human figure varying in line quality (smooth to sketchy) and in articulation (few details to many details). All the thirty-six possible pairings of the drawings were presented, one pair at a time, and the children were asked to say how similar they thought each pair of drawings was. Subsequently, the children were again presented with the same thirty-six pairings, but this time asked to indicate which member of each pair they liked best.

The results indicated that even four-year-olds were sensitive to articulation and to line quality, as expressed in their preference judgements. On the similarity judgements, children of all ages employed articulation as their primary criterion. The use of simple and interesting test material (a human figure) may have been partly responsible for the greater apparent sensitivity of the procedures used by Itskowitz *et al.* over those employed by Carothers and Gardner.

There is also evidence to support the view that children have preferences for certain patterns and shapes. Several early studies, reviewed by Harris (1963), have indicated that children have preferences for balanced and symmetrical compositions, but such preferences were clearly evident only in judgements made by older children (eight years and over). As in the study by Carothers and Gardner (1979) children appeared to be sensitive to aesthetic properties in drawings made by others before they were able to produce these properties in their own work.

Some more recent work suggests that compositional preferences may be present even in infancy. Bornstein, Ferdinandsen and Gross (1981) have found that four-month-old infants process vertically symmetrical patterns more efficiently than horizontally symmetrical or asymmetrical ones. Although the four-month-old infants showed no preference for symmetry, twelve-month-old infants preferred vertical symmetry to horizontal symmetry and asymmetry. (Preference was measured by comparing the time infants spent looking at each of the patterns presented). These and subsequent results (see Bornstein and Stiles-Davis, 1984) indicate that vertical symmetry has a special status in early perceptual development. Bornstein *et al.* (1981) were not able to decide whether this special status was innate or based on experience. They did suggest, however, that it might derive from the vertical symmetry of the human figure when viewed from the front. We have here, therefore, the beginnings of the body of evidence that will be required to substantiate the claim that there are certain visual forms with a universal appeal (see Arnheim, 1956; Kellogg, 1970; Goodnow, 1977; Gardner, 1980; Winner, 1982). It goes almost without saying that much empirical work remains to be done on this question.

Children's understanding of art

In one of the few studies of children's understanding of art, Gardner and Winner (1976) asked children aged between four and twelve years a number of questions about a picture, a poem or some music. The questions concerned such matters as the way in which art is produced ("Where do you think this came from?"), sensitivity of style ("How can you tell if two paintings were made by different artists?"), the relation of a picture to the topic depicted ("What is the difference between a real shell and a painting of a shell?"), and evaluation ("Do you like it? How can you decide if it is good?").

On the basis of their results, Gardner and Winner concluded that children pass through three stages in their understanding of art. The youngest children, aged four to seven years, thought that paintings probably come from a factory and showed little awareness that people need special talent and skills to make a good painting. These same children usually confused the picture with the thing it depicted. They said that a Goya equestrian painting was "a horse" rather than "a painting of a horse". Interestingly, and consistently with this result, Haber (1980) reports that children, unlike adults, are usually quite insensitive perceptually to a picture as a surface. In general, these youngest children did not express opinions about the quality of a work of art and did not agree on what makes a painting good. Some children thought all opinions equally valid, others thought that art evaluations should come from authority such as parents or teachers. Many of the youngest children preferred abstract paintings to realistic pictures.

Children aged seven to ten years, in contrast, showed a strong preference for visual realism in paintings. They were also more aware of differences between a picture and the topic depicted. They were sensitive to style, but considered that the main purpose of art was to make exact copies. Not surprisingly, the oldest children interviewed – the adolescents – were more like adults in their understanding of art. They recognized the possibility of many different ways and styles of creating art and understood more of its symbolic and expressive aspects. The oldest and youngest children were alike, however, in not recognizing any set of aesthetic standards that could be used to evaluate art. The evaluation of art for most of the adolescents was just a matter of personal taste.

This pattern of results does not give much support to the notion that young children have an awareness of adult art. If anything, it rather looks as if some understanding of art is only acquired gradually as children get older.

Art education

In this book we have reviewed many aspects of the drawing process and argued that constructing a drawing is a complex task with cognitive, design, planning and performance factors all playing an important role. We would like now to consider whether there are any implications of the analyses reviewed here for the teaching of drawing to children. We are concerned here only with the production of drawings and not with children's perceptions and understanding of art.

There are two major views on the teaching of drawing (and art generally). Traditional psychological approaches to children's drawing lead to the conclusion that little should be attempted in the way of formal teaching of graphic techniques to children. Many developmental psychologists, such as Harris (1963) and Piaget (Piaget and Inhelder, 1969), who have dominated traditional thinking about children's drawing, gave little attention to the drawing process. The implication of this view is that no teaching in drawing is necessary, because as children grow older their maturing cognitive abilities will automatically result in more developmentally advanced mental images, which in turn will be translated into "better" pictures.

In recent years, some art educators have taken a somewhat different line, but with much the same conclusion at the end – that the teaching of specific drawing techniques is not necessary. Art educators such as Lowenfeld have, for the most part, identified individual self-expression as the main value of drawing and other artistic activities. They have also assumed that teaching children how to use graphic devices and formulas to make their pictures will inhibit children from using their art for self-expression. Consequently, they have warned that children should be discouraged from copying pictures and drawings (see, for example, Lowenfeld, 1947). Similarly, Arnheim (1956) claimed that by copying pictures made by others, children do not learn how to create order in their own drawings. And according to Kellogg (1970), a child should not be encouraged to copy, because a copied figure may quickly become a stereotyped formula and result in a loss of interest in drawing.

Thus, traditional developmental psychology and some authorities on art education all seem to indicate that a facilitative, but essentially non-directive *laisser-faire* approach may be the most appropriate educational practice with regard to children's drawing. The advice from this tradition is not to encourage copying.

The history of art, however, suggests that a totally different kind of art education may be required, especially for older children. Historically, artists were craftsmen and learned their craft as apprentices. They were explicitly taught techniques and drawing devices as procedures. Gombrich (1972) describes the pattern books and manuals which Renaissance artists produced in large numbers to encourage the training of apprentices and the development of their art. The basis of all these books was that you could learn *how to draw* a "man", a "horse", and so forth by copying patterns or formulas which had been discovered/invented by earlier masters. The manuals contained page after page of patterns for an immense range of topics seen from all angles. Thus, for example, there would be formulas and patterns for ears and eyes, for mouths and noses of all conceivable shapes and sizes. These formulas and the copying exercises were not regarded as short-cuts or tricks of the trade, but as necessary procedures for acquiring the skills for successful picture making. Victorian art education embodied an essentially similar approach.

It may be, therefore, that copying is not as harmful as some modern authorities have supposed. Gardner (1980), for example, has pointed out that copying may also play a formative role in the achievement of artistry, in that it is a means of achieving more accurate representation. Some research suggests that children will copy anyway, regardless of what attitude their teachers take. Wilson and Wilson (1977) surveyed the drawings made by a large number of adolescents and found that nearly every drawing could be traced back to some pre-existing image which the drawer had copied. On the basis of these results, Wilson and Wilson also concluded that copying may be beneficial. They argued that young children are initially capable of developing their own artistic activities using their own resources, but that these resources will finally become insufficient. If older children are to develop further artistically, they may need the additional support to be gained from copying the graphic material available in their environment. The borrowed graphic schemata, once located, may then be adapted and elaborated in the children's own drawings.

Should children, then, be allowed to copy in their drawing? Duncum (1988) suggested that those who have been most against copying have tended to see children's drawing as art in which self-expression is important, whereas those who see a role for copying have been more concerned with children's acquisition of techniques. The available evidence, in our view, suggests that it may be important to encourage children to develop their own solutions to graphic problems, while not preventing them altogether from copying new graphic formulas which they can adapt in their own work.

Summary

It is often held that art is characterized by three properties – repleteness, expression and composition. Drawings made by very young children are often artistically appealing to adults, but there is less evidence that children who make such appealing drawings actually apply artistic criteria to their own work. Research has found no evidence that young children are aware of the properties of expression and repleteness in their own or other people's drawings. There is, however, some evidence that even infants are sensitive to composition. Ironically, understanding of art as a cultural phenomenon is typically found only in older children, whose drawings are usually aesthetically uninteresting to most adults.

10 Conclusions and future directions

The psychology of children's drawings covers an unusually wide range of approaches and interests. In this book we have scarcely been able to do justice to even a limited selection of the thousands of reports, chapters and books on the subject. We hope, however, that we have provided a sufficiently comprehensive introduction to identify the main landmarks of this field of study. We hope, also, that there are sufficient references to give interested readers access to the original material.

Inevitably, our selection of topics for discussion has reflected our own interests and there have been gaps in our account of children's drawing. We have hardly mentioned, for example, children's attempts to portray action and activities in their drawing (see Arnheim, 1956; Lowenfeld, 1947). Furthermore, in our discussion of children's drawings as art, we have perhaps too readily treated drawing in isolation as if it were the only medium of artistic expression for children and have ignored possible relations between drawing and other art forms such as painting, modelling and sculpture (see Golomb, 1973). Similarly, we have only briefly touched upon sex- and cross-cultural differences in children's drawing.

In writing this book we have become aware that there are also some gaps in past and present research into children's drawing. First, almost without exception, children's drawing has been studied from an adult point of view. We know very little of what children themselves think about their own drawings and that of others. Without doubt, it can be difficult to investigate children's verbal reactions to drawings in a reliable and systematic way (Freeman, 1980), but the effort to do so may be worthwhile. Progress in our understanding of children's expression of emotion in drawing, for example, may depend on studying children's perceptions of pictures as well as their production of drawings.

A second gap in past research concerns the drawings of children younger than four years. The drawing of these children has not been completely neglected (see, for example, Kellogg, 1970), but there have been fewer analytical studies to probe their capabilities than have been carried out on older children. Further investigation of the drawing of younger children may prove to be rewarding. There are interesting signs, for example, that even three-year-olds can produce relatively sophisticated graphic representations with visually-realistic elements. This has important implications for our theoretical understanding of children's drawing development.

These minor points notwithstanding, the main themes in the study of children's drawing should now be clear. One striking feature of the subject area is that since the early studies of Luquet, Goodenough, and others, the study of drawing lost its once central position in child psychology and increasingly became very much a minor specialism. By the 1970s, for example, children's drawing was not mentioned at all in many textbooks on child psychology or child development. The reasons for the omission of drawing from these textbooks most probably lay in its relative lack of significance for the developmental theories of Piaget and his followers.

It should now be apparent, however, that the study of children's drawing is currently undergoing something of a renaissance. This renewal of interest has undoubtedly arisen from the recognition of the complexity of the process of executing a drawing (Freeman, 1980). Our belated appreciation of the importance of this process has had several important consequences:

1. The developmental significance of children's performance on a variety of drawing tasks has been quite transformed.
2. Our theoretical understanding of children's drawing itself has been significantly advanced.
3. Lines of enquiry which had previously seemed uninviting now offer the promise of orderly data and reliable conclusions.

Three areas of child psychology, in particular, seem set to gain from further study of drawing: the psychology of emotional expression, the psychology of writing and the psychology of thinking.

Expression of emotion

As we have noted in Chapter 7, children's drawings have often been analysed in attempts to assess personality and emotional adjustment. Unfortunately, much of the early work can be criticized for the subjectivity of the assessments and for the lack of adequate controls. Furthermore, interpretation of the results of many otherwise well-conducted studies is problematic because the effects of emotional significance were confounded with performance factors related to the drawing process (see Chapter 7). Recently, however, adequately controlled studies (which take performance factors into account) have begun to yield new evidence that there may be valid general principles which can be applied to the interpretation of emotional expression in drawings (see, for example, Thomas, Chaigne and Fox, in press). If these findings are repeated with clinically anxious populations, then we may see real improvements in the use of drawings for the assessment of emotional adjustment and anxiety.

Drawing and early writing

Learning to write is undoubtedly one of the most important accomplishments for children in their first years at school. The accomplishment of writing requires children both to learn to draw letters accurately and to combine letters together in words and sentences to convey meaning. We are still some way from an adequate theory of mature adult writing (see Hayes and Flower, 1986), let alone a theory of the acquisition of writing skills by young children. Current educational practice is to teach writing once children have started to learn to read and to assume substantial transfer of skill from reading to writing. Apart from some work by Goodnow (1977) on children's production of the shapes needed to form letters, the accepted view seems to be that children's drawing experience is largely irrelevant to writing. Donaldson (1984), for example, has implied that an interest in drawing may actually interfere with learning to write if it discourages children from considering other means of representation.

We do not wish to suggest here that the current strategy of linking the teaching of writing to that of reading is unsound. There are, however, good reasons to think that writing requires significant skills in addition to those involved in reading. It also seems plausible that there will be many similarities between early writing and children's drawing; both activities are directed at graphic representation and it seems likely that children may encounter somewhat similar problems in both. Specifically, current analyses of children's drawing that stress the problems of planning, sequencing and satisfying multiple constraints seem to us to be very similar to contemporary analyses of (adult) writing (see, for example, Flower and Hayes, 1980). That said, detailed exploration of possible links between drawing and early writing remains a matter for future research.

Drawing and thinking

One of the most striking recent developments in the study of children's drawing has been the realization that making a drawing is a complex achievement and not just an effortless projection of conceptual knowledge onto a sheet of paper. As Freeman (1980) has amply documented, drawing a picture requires considerable cognitive work for its successful accomplishment. Having recognized that drawing is a product of thinking, as it were, we are now in a position to contemplate the further possibility that drawing may actually facilitate thinking.

The idea that pictures might facilitate thinking is not new. Arnheim (1969) was firmly convinced that all thinking is basically perceptual in nature and argued for the recognition that much thinking involves images. The involvement of images in thinking is indicated also in Paivio's dual coding theory which proposes the coding of information in one of two distinct forms – verbal or imaginal (Paivio, 1971). We need take no stand here on the question of whether one form of coding is better or more fundamental than the other. Arnheim's important point is that if some thinking, at least, involves images, then appropriate visual experience will be essential for effective education (Arnheim, 1969).

We would like to take this argument one step further and suggest that in addition to visual experience of images and pictures made by others, there may be benefits to children from engaging in drawing themselves. Two sorts of benefit seem possible: first, there may be a helpful effect on general cognitive development. There are several possible ways in which this hypothesis could be investigated. We might look, for example, for evidence that children amply provided with opportunities for drawing might perform better in assessments of scholastic ability and intelligence. While long-lasting effects of drawing on intellectual ability cannot be ruled out, we think that such effects might be hard to detect. In any case, the *ex post facto* design of studies to investigate such questions makes it difficult to draw firm conclusions about cause and effect.

The second possible benefit from drawing is that it may help children solve particular problems; that is to say, drawing may facilitate thinking. This notion is similar to the suggestion that, for adults, writing can be an aid to thinking. Many recent conceptualizations of writing have stressed that writing is often more than the mere expression of preconceived meaning in words, and can be an important part of the thinking process (see, for example, Wason, 1970; Elbow, 1973; Collins and Gentner, 1980; Flower and Hayes, 1980). If writing can facilitate thinking about ideas and information coded verbally, then it is plausible that drawing can facilitate thinking about ideas coded in images.

Is there any reason to believe this suggestion? Engineers and craftsmen, of course, often make sketches and working drawings to aid their planning and design work. There is also historical evidence that skill at drawing often accompanied scientific discovery and technical invention (see Edgerton, 1980).

If adult thinking can be facilitated by drawing, then it seems reasonable to ask whether thinking and problem-solving in children might also be facilitated by drawing. A possible line of research would be to investigate children's problem-solving as it occurs and determine whether or not encouraging children to sketch out possible solutions results in more diverse and creative thinking.

A final word

Many of our thoughts about future directions are, to be completely frank, rather speculative, and we shall not be very surprised if our detailed predictions turn out to be wide of the mark. Nevertheless, we remain convinced that children's drawing is an activity of hitherto neglected developmental significance. Our grounds for considering drawing to be significant are that it is a cognitively complex activity which many children find absorbing and practise extensively. It may be that the effects of individual drawing exercises in fostering competence may not always be easy to detect. Nevertheless, the cumulative effects of drawing, together with other forms of play, may be crucially important in the development of early intelligence and later competence in a variety of activities (see Bruner, 1972). We are fortunate that there are so many promising lines of enquiry to pursue. Only time and further work will tell which turn out to be the most productive.

References

Alland, A. (1983) *Playing with Form*, New York: Columbia University Press.

Allik, J. and Laak, T. (1985) "The head is smaller than the body: But how does it join on?", in Freeman, N. H. and Cox, M. V. (eds) *Visual Order*, Cambridge: Cambridge University Press.

American Psychiatric Association, *Diagnostic and Statistical Manual of Mental Disorders* (1st edn, 1952; 2nd edn, 1968; 3rd edn, 1980), Washington DC: APA.

Anastasi, A. (1976) *Psychological Testing* (4th edn), New York: Collier-Macmillan.

Anastasi, A. and Foley, J. Jr (1936) "An analysis of spontaneous drawings by children in different cultures", *Journal of Applied Psychology*, 20, 689–726.

Arnheim, R. (1956) *Art and Visual Perception: A Psychology of the Creative Eye*, London: Faber & Faber.

Arnheim, R. (1967) *Toward a Psychology of Art*, Berkeley: University of California Press.

Arnheim, R. (1969) *Visual Thinking*, London: Faber & Faber.

Arnheim, R. (1971) "On information available in pictures", *Leonardo*, 4, 197.

Arnheim, R. (1974) *Art and Visual Perception: A Psychology of the Creative Eye. The New Version*, Berkeley and Los Angeles: University of California Press.

Arnheim, R. (1980) "The puzzle of Nadia's drawings", *The Arts in Psychotherapy*, 7, 79–85.

Ballard, P. B. (1912) "What London children like to draw", *Journal of Experimental Pedagogy*, 1, 185–97.

Barkan, M. (1955) *A Foundation for Art Education*, New York: Ronald Press Co.

Barnhart, E. N. (1942) "Developmental stages in compositional construction in children's drawings", *Journal of Experimental Education*, 11, 156–81.

Barrett, M. D. and Light, P. H. (1976) "Symbolism and intellectual realism in children's drawings", *British Journal of Educational*

Psychology, 46, 198-202.

Beardsley, M. (1958) *Aesthetics: Problems in the Philosophy of Criticism*, New York: Harcourt Brace.

Beardsley, M. (1979) "In defense of aesthetic value", *Proceedings and Addresses of the American Philosophical Association*, 723-49.

Bender, L. (1938) "A visual motor Gestalt test and its clinical use", *Research Monograph No. 3*, American Orthopsychiatric Association.

Bergin, A. E. (1971) "The evaluation of therapeutic outcomes", in Bergin, A. E. and Garfield, S. L. *Handbook of Psychotherapy and Behavior Change: An Empirical Analysis*, New York: John Wiley.

Bergin, A. E. (1975) "Psychotherapy can be dangerous", *Psychology Today*, 9, (6), 96-104.

Blank, P., Massey, C., Gardner, H. and Winner, E. (1984) "Perceiving what paintings express", in Crozier, W. R. and Chapman, A. J. (eds) *Cognitive Processes in the Perception of Art*, Amsterdam: Elsevier Science Publishers.

Bornstein, M. H., Ferdinandsen, K. and Gross, C. G. (1981) "Perception of symmetry in infancy", *Developmental Psychology*, 17, 82-6.

Bornstein, M. H. and Stiles-Davis, J. (1984) "Discrimination and memory for symmetry in young children", *Developmental Psychology*, 20, 637-49.

Bremner, J. G. (1985) "Figural biases and young children's drawings", in Freeman, N. H. and Cox, M. V. (eds) *Visual Order*, Cambridge: Cambridge University Press.

Bremner, J. G. and Moore, S. (1984) "Prior visual inspection and object naming: Two factors that enhance hidden feature inclusion in young children's drawings", *British Journal of Developmental Psychology*, 2, 371-6.

Bremner, J. G. and Taylor, A. J. (1982) "Children's errors in copying angles: Perpendicular error or bisection error?", *Perception*, 11, 163-71.

Britsch, G. (1926) *Theorie der Bildenden Kunst*, Munich: F. Bruckman.

Bruner, J. (1972) "Nature and uses of immaturity", *American Psychologist*, 27, 1-28.

Buck, J. N. (1948) "The HTP test", *Journal of Clinical Psychology*, 4, 151-9.

Cabe, P. A. (1980) "Picture perception in nonhuman subjects", in Hagen, M. A. (ed.) *The Perception of Pictures*, Vol. 2, New York: Academic Press.

Carothers, T. and Gardner, H. (1979) "When children's drawings become art: The emergence of aesthetic production and perception", *Developmental Psychology*, 15, 570-80.

Clark, A. B. (1897) "The child's attitude towards perspective problems", in E. Barnes (ed.), *Studies in Education*, Vol. I, Stanford: Stanford University Press.

Collins, A. and Gentner, D. (1980) "A framework for a cognitive theory of writing", in Gregg, L. W. and Steinberg, E. R (eds) *Cognitive Processes in Writing*, Hillsdale, N.J.: Lawrence Erlbaum Associates.

Costall, A. (1985) "How meaning covers the traces", in Freeman, N. H. and Cox, M. V. (eds) *Visual Order*, Cambridge: Cambridge University Press.

Cox, M. V. (1978) "Spatial depth relationships in young children's drawings", *Journal of Experimental Child Psychology*, 26, 551-4.

Cox, M. V. (1980) *Are Young Children Egocentric?*, London: Batsford Academic.

Cox, M. V. (1981) "One thing behind another: Problems of representation in children's drawings", *Educational Psychology*, 1, (4), 275-87.

Cox, M. V. (1985) "One object behind another: Young children's use of array-specific or view-specific representations", in Freeman, N. H. and Cox, M. V. (eds) *Visual Order*, Cambridge: Cambridge University Press.

Cox, M. V. (1986a) *The Child's Point of View*, Hemel Hempstead: Harvester Wheatsheaf.

Cox, M. V. (1986b) "Cubes are difficult things to draw", *British Journal of Developmental Psychology*, 4, 341-5.

Craddick, R. A. (1961) "Size of Santa Claus drawings as a function of the time before and after Christmas", *Journal of Psychological Studies*, 12, 121-5.

Craddick, R. A. (1963) "Size of Halloween witch drawings prior to, on and after Halloween", *Perceptual and Motor Skills*, 16, 235-8.

Crook, C. K. (1984) "Factors influencing the use of transparency in children's drawing", *British Journal of Developmental Psychology*, 2, 213-21.

Crook, C. (1985) "Knowledge and appearance" in Freeman, N. H., and Cox, M. V. (eds) *Visual Order*, Cambridge: Cambridge University Press.

Dalley, T. (1984) "Introduction", in Dalley, T. (ed.) *Art as Therapy*, London: Tavistock Publications.

Davis, A. M. (1983) "Contextual sensitivity in young children's drawings", *Journal of Experimental Child Psychology*, 35, 478-86.

Davis, A. M. (1984) "Noncanonical orientation without occlusion: Children's drawings of transparent objects", *Journal of Experimental Child Psychology*, 37, 451-62.

Davison, G. C. and Neale, J. M. (1982) *Abnormal Psychology* (3rd edn), New York: John Wiley.

Deregowski, J. B. (1970) "Note on the possible determinants of 'split-representation' as an artistic style", *International Journal of Psychology*, 5, 21–6.

Deregowski, J. B. (1977) "Pictures, symbols and frames of reference", in Butterworth, G. E. (ed.) *The Child's Representation of the World*, New York: Plenum.

Deregowski, J. B. (1980) *Illusions, Patterns and Pictures: A Cross-Cultural Perspective*, London: Academic Press.

Deregowski, J. B. (1984) *Distortion in Art: The Eye and the Mind*, London: Routledge & Kegan Paul.

Diagnostic and Statistical Manual of Mental Disorders (1st edn, 1952; 2nd edn, 1968; 3rd edn, 1980), Washington DC: American Psychiatric Association.

Dickie, G. (1985) "Evaluating art", *British Journal of Aesthetics*, 25, (1), 3–16.

Di Leo, J. H. (1970) *Young Children and their Drawings*, New York: Brunner/Mazel Publishers.

Donaldson, M. (1978) *Children's Minds*, London: Fontana.

Donaldson, M. (1984) "Speech and writing and modes of learning", in Goelman, H., Oberg, A. and Smith, F. (eds) *Awakening to Literacy*, London: Heinemann.

Duncum, P. (1988) "To copy or not to copy: A review", *Studies in Art Education*, 29 (4), 203–10.

Ecker, D. W. (1976) "The critical act in aesthetic inquiry", in Eisner, E. W. (ed.) *The Arts, Human Development, and Education*, Berkeley, Cal.: McCutchan Publishing Corporation.

Edgerton, S. Y. Jr (1980) "The Renaissance artist as quantifier", in Hagen, M. A. (ed.) *The Perception of Pictures*, Vol. 1, New York: Academic Press.

Efland, A. D. (1976) "Changing views of children's artistic development: Their impact on curriculum and instruction", in Eisner, E. W. (ed.) *The Arts, Human Development, and Education*, Berkeley, Cal.: McCutchan Publishing Corporation.

Eisner, E. W. (1972) *Educating Artistic Vision*, New York: Macmillan.

Elbow, P. (1973) *Writing Without Teachers*, Oxford: Oxford University Press.

Eng, H. (1931) *The Psychology of Children's Drawings*, London: Routledge & Kegan Paul.

Erikson, E. H. (1968) *Identity: Youth and Crisis*, New York: Norton.

Fenson, L. (1985) "The transition from construction to sketching in children's drawings", in Freeman, N. H. and Cox, M. V. (eds) *Visual Order*, Cambridge: Cambridge University Press.

Ferreiro, E. (1985) "Literacy development: A psychogenetic perspective", in Olson, D. R., Torrance, N. and Hildyard, A. (eds) *Literacy, Language, and Learning: The Nature and Consequences of Reading and Writing*, Cambridge: Cambridge University Press.

Flower, L. S. and Hayes, J. (1980) "The dynamics of composing: Making plans and juggling constraints", in Gregg, L. W. and Steinberg, E. R. (eds) *Cognitive Processes in Writing*, Hillsdale, N.J.: Lawrence Erlbaum Associates.

Fox, T. (1989) "Some effects of emotional significance of the topic on the size of children's drawings", unpublished Masters thesis, University of Birmingham.

Fox, T. and Thomas, G. V. (in press) "Children's drawings of an anxiety-eliciting topic: Effects on the size of the drawing", *British Journal of Clinical Psychology*.

Freeman, N. H. (1972) "Process and product in children's drawing", *Perception*, 1, 123–40.

Freeman, N. H. (1976) "Children's drawings: Cognitive aspects", *Journal of Child Psychology and Psychiatry*, 17, 345–50.

Freeman, N. H. (1980) *Strategies of Representation in Young Children: Analysis of Spatial Skills and Drawing Processes*, London: Academic Press.

Freeman, N. H. (1986) "How should a cube be drawn?", *British Journal of Developmental Psychology*, 4, 317–22.

Freeman, N. H. (1987) "Current problems in the development of representational picture-production", *Archives de Psychologie*, 55, 127–52.

Freeman, N. H. and Cox, M. V. (eds) (1985) *Visual Order*, Cambridge: Cambridge University Press.

Freeman, N. H., Eiser, C. and Sayers, J. (1977) "Children's strategies in producing 3-D relationships on a 2-D surface", *Journal of Experimental Child Psychology*, 23, 305–14.

Freeman, N. H. and Hargreaves, S. (1977) "Directed movements and the body-proportion effect in pre-school children's human figure drawings", *Quarterly Journal of Experimental Psychology*, 29, 227–35.

Freeman, N. H. and Janikoun, R. (1972) "Intellectual realism in children's drawings of a familiar object with distinct features", *Child Development*, 43, 1,116–21.

Freud, S. (1976) *Introductory Lectures on Psychoanalysis* (translated by J. Strachey; edited by J. Strachey and A. Richards), Harmondsworth, Middlesex: Penguin Books.

Friedman, S. L. and Stevenson, M. B. (1980) "Perception of movement in pictures", in Hagen M. A. (ed.) *The Perception of Pictures*, Vol. 1. New York: Academic Press.

Frisby, J. P (1979) *Seeing: Illusion, Brain and Mind*, Oxford: Oxford University Press.

Gardner, H. (1973) *The Arts and Human Development*, New York: John Wiley.

Gardner, H. (1980) *Artful Scribbles: The Significance of Children's Drawings*, New York: Basic Books.

Gardner, H. and Winner, E. (1976) "Three stages of understanding art", *Psychology Today*, 9, (10), 42–5, 74.

Gibson, J. J. (1950) *The Perception of the Visual World*, Boston: Houghton Mifflin.

Gibson, J. J. (1979) *The Ecological Approach to Visual Perception*, Boston: Houghton Mifflin.

Gibson, J. J. (1980) "Foreword: A prefatory essay on the perception of surfaces versus the perception of markings on a surface", in Hagen, M. A. (ed.) *The Perception of Pictures*, Vol. 1, New York: Academic Press.

Golomb, C. (1973) "Children's representation of the human figure: The effects of models, media and instruction", *Genetic Psychology Monographs*, 87, 197–251.

Golomb, C. (1974) *Young Children's Sculpture and Drawing*, Cambridge, Mass.: Harvard University Press.

Gombrich, E. H. (1971) "On information available in pictures", *Leonardo*, 4, 195–7.

Gombrich, E. H. (1972) *Art and Illusion: A Study in the Psychology of Pictorial Representation* (4th edn), London: Phaidon Press.

Gombrich, E. H. (1982) *The Image and the Eye*, Oxford: Phaidon Press.

Goodenough, F. L. (1926) *Measurement of Intelligence by Drawings*, New York: Harcourt, Brace & World.

Goodman, N. (1968) *Languages of Art*, Indianapolis: Bobbs-Merrill.

Goodman, N. (1976) *Languages of Art* (2nd edn), Indianapolis: Hackett.

Goodnow, J. J. (1972) "Rules and repertoires, rituals and tricks of the trade: Social and informational aspects to cognitive and representational development", in Farham-Diggory, S. (ed.) *Information Processing in Children*, New York: Academic Press.

Goodnow, J. (1977) *Children's Drawing*, Cambridge, Mass.: Harvard University Press.

Goodnow, J. J. and Friedman, S. (1972) "Orientation in children's human figure drawings: An aspect of graphic language", *Developmental Psychology*, 7, 10–16.

Goodnow, J. J. and Levine, R. A. (1973) "The grammar of action: Sequence and syntax in children's copying", *Cognitive Psychology*, 4, 82–98.

Goodwin, J. (1982) "Use of drawings in evaluating children who may be incest victims", *Children and Youth Services Review*, 4, 269–78.

Graewe, H. (1935) "Das Tierzeichnen der Kinder", *Zeitschrift für Pädagogische Psychologie*, 36, 25–256, 291–300.

Gregory, R. L. (1966) *Eye and Brain*, London: Weidenfeld and Nicolson.

Gregory, R. L. (1970) *The Intelligent Eye*, London: Weidenfeld and Nicolson.

Groos, K. (1901) *The Play of Man*, New York: Appleton.

Haber, R. N. (1979) "Twenty years of haunting eidetic imagery: Where's the ghost?", *The Behavioral and Brain Sciences*, 2, 583–629.

Haber, R. N. (1980) "Perceiving space from pictures: A theoretical analysis", in Hagen M. A. (ed.) *The Perception of Pictures*, Vol. 1., New York: Academic Press.

Hagen, M. A. (1976) "Picture perception: Toward a theoretical model", *Psychological Bulletin*, 81, 471–97.

Hagen, M. A. (1980a) "Introduction: What, then, are pictures?", in Hagen, M. A. (ed.) *The Perception of Pictures*, Vol. 1., New York: Academic Press.

Hagen, M. A. (1980b) "Generative theory: A perceptual theory of pictorial representation", in Hagen M. A. (ed.) *The Perception of Pictures*, Vol. 2. New York: Academic Press.

Hagen, M. A. (1985) "There is no development in art", in Freeman, N. H. and Cox, M. V. (eds) *Visual Order*, Cambridge: Cambridge University Press.

Hagen, M. A. and Jones, R. K. (1978) "Cultural effects on pictorial perception: How many words is one picture really worth?" in Walk, R. D. and Pick, H. L. (eds) *Perception and Experience*, New York: Plenum Press.

Hall, G. S. (1906) *Youth*, New York: Appleton

Hammer, E. F. (1953) "Frustration-aggression hypothesis extended to socio-racial areas: Comparison of Negro and white children's H-T-P's", *Psychiatric Quarterly*, 27, 597–607.

Hammer, E. F. (1958) *The Clinical Application of Projective Drawings*, Springfield, Ill.: C. C. Thomas.

Harris, D. B. (1963) *Children's Drawings as Measures of Intellectual Maturity*, New York: Harcourt, Brace & World.

Hayes, J. R. and Flower, L. S. (1986) "Writing research and the writer", *American Psychologist*, 41, 1106–13.

Henderson, J. A. and Thomas, G. V. (1988) "Looking ahead: Planning for the inclusion of detail affects relative sizes of head and trunk in children's human figure drawings", unpublished manuscript.

Hochberg, J. (1970) "The representation of things and people", in

Gombrich, E. H., Hochberg, J. and Black, M. (eds) *Art Perception and Reality*, Baltimore, Md.: Johns Hopkins University Press.

Hochberg, J. (1978) *Perception* (2nd edn), Englewood Cliffs, N.J.: Prentice-Hall.

Hochberg, J. and Brooks, V. (1962) "Pictorial recognition as an unlearned ability: A study of one child's performance", *American Journal of Psychology*, 73, 624–8.

Howe, M. J. A. and Smith, J. (1988) "Calendar calculating in 'idiots savants': How do they do it?", *British Journal of Psychology*, 79 (3), 371–86.

Ibbotson, A. and Bryant, P. E. (1976) "The perpendicular error and the vertical effect", *Perception*, 5, 319–26.

Ilg, F. L. and Ames, L. B. (1965) *School Readiness*, New York: Harper & Row.

Ingram, N. and Butterworth, G. (1989) "The young child's representation of depth in drawing: Process and product", *Journal of Experimental Child Psychology*, 47, 356–69.

Itskowitz, R., Glaubman, H. and Hoffman, M, (1988) "The impact of age and artistic inclination on the use of articulation and line quality in similarity and preference judgements", *Journal of Experimental Child Psychology*, 46, 21–34.

Ives, S. W. (1980) "The use of orientations in children's drawings of familiar objects: Principles versus percepts", *British Journal of Educational Psychology*, 50, 295–6.

Ives, S. W. and Rovet, J. (1979) "The role of graphic orientations in children's drawings of familiar and novel objects, at rest and in motion", *Merrill Palmer Quarterly*, 25, 281–92.

Jones, R. K. and Hagen, M. A. (1980) "A perspective on cross-cultural picture perception", in Hagen M. A. (ed.) *The Perception of Pictures*, Vol. 2, New York: Academic Press.

Kanner, L. (1943) "Autistic disturbances of affective contact", *Nervous Child*, 2, 217–50.

Kellogg, R. (1970) *Analysing Children's Art*, Palo Alto, Cal.: National Press Books.

Kennedy, J. M. (1974) *A Psychology of Picture Perception: Information and Images*, San Francisco: Jossey-Bass.

Kennedy, J. M. (1980) "Blind people recognizing and making haptic pictures", in Hagen, M. A. (ed.) *The Perception of Pictures*, Vol. II, New York: Academic Press.

Kerschensteiner, G. (1905) *Die Entwicklung der Zeichnerischen Begabung*, Munich: Carl Gerber.

Kohler, W. (1929) *Gestalt Psychology*, New York: Liveright.

Koppitz, E. (1968) *Psychological Evaluation of Children's Human Figure Drawings*, London: Grune & Stratton.

Koppitz, E. (1984) *Psychological Evaluation of Human Figure Drawings by Middle School Pupils*, London: Grune & Stratton.

Lark-Horovitz, B., Lewis, H. and Luca, M. (1967) *Understanding Children's Art for Better Teaching*, Columbus, Ohio: Merrill.

Levy, J. (1978) *Play Behavior*, New York: John Wiley.

Levy, S. and Levy, R. A. (1958) "Symbolism in animal drawings", in Hammer, E. F. (ed.) *The Clinical Application of Projective Drawings*, Springfield, Ill.: C. C. Thomas.

Light, P. H. (1985) "The development of view-specific representation considered from a socio-cognitive standpoint", in Freeman, N. H. and Cox, M. V. (eds) *Visual Order*, Cambridge: Cambridge University Press.

Light, P. H. and Foot, T. (1986) "Partial occlusion in young children's drawings", *Journal of Experimental Child Psychology*, 41, 38–48.

Light, P. H. and Humphreys, J. (1981) "Internal relationships in young children's drawings", *Journal of Experimental Child Psychology*, 31, 521–30.

Light, P. H. and MacIntosh, E. (1980) "Depth relationships in young children's drawings", *Journal of Experimental Child Psychology*, 30, 79–87.

Light, P. H. and Simmons, B. (1983) "The effects of a communication task upon the representation of depth relationships in young children's drawings", *Journal of Experimental Child Psychology*, 35 (1), 81–92.

Lowenfeld, V. (1939) *The Nature of Creative Activity*, New York: Macmillan.

Lowenfeld, V. (1947) *Creative and Mental Growth*, New York: Macmillan.

Lowenfeld, V. and Brittain, W. L. (1975) *Creative and Mental Growth* (6th edn compiled by W. L. Brittain), London: Collier-Macmillan.

Lukens, H. (1896) "A study of children's drawings in the early years", *Pedagogical Seminar*, 4, 79–110.

Luquet, G. H. (1913) *Les Dessins d'un enfant*, Paris: Alcan.

Luquet, G. H. (1927) *Le Dessin Enfantin*, Paris: Alcan.

Machover, K. (1949) *Personality Projection in the Drawings of the Human Figure*, Springfield, Ill.: C. C. Thomas.

Mackavey, W. A. (1980) "Exceptional cases of pictorial perspective", in Hagen, M. A. (ed.) *The Perception of Pictures*, Vol. 1, New York: Academic Press.

Maitland, L. (1895) "What children draw to please themselves", *Inland Educator*, 1, 119–25.

Marr, D. (1977) "Analysis of occluding contour", *Proceedings of the Royal Society, London*, series B, 197, 411–75.

Marr, D. (1982) *Vision*, San Francisco: Freeman.

Martindale, C. (1984) "The evolution of aesthetic taste", in Gergen, K. J. and Gergen, M. M. (eds) *Historical Social Psychology*, Hillsdale, NJ.: Lawrence Erlbaum Associates.

Moore, V. (1985) "The use of a colouring task to elucidate children's drawings of a solid cube", *British Journal of Developmental Psychology*, 4, 335–40.

Moore, V. (1987) "The influence of experience on children's drawings of a familiar and unfamiliar object", *British Journal of Developmental Psychology*, 5, (3), 221–9.

Morishima, A. (1974) "Another Van Gogh of Japan: The superior artwork of a retarded boy", *Exceptional Children*, 41, 92–6.

Morris, D. (1967) *The Biology of Art*, Chicago: Aldine-Atherton.

Nunnally, J. C. (1978) *Psychometric Theory* (2nd edn), New York: McGraw-Hill.

O'Connor, N. and Hermelin, B. (1987a) "Visual memory and motor programmes: Their use by idiot-savant artists and controls", *British Journal of Psychology*, 78, 307–23.

O'Connor, N. and Hermelin, B. (1987b) "Visual and graphic abilities of the idiot-savant artist", *Psychological Medicine*, 17, 81–92.

Olsen, D. R. (1970) *Cognitive Development: The Child's Acquisition of Diagonality*, New York and London: Academic Press.

Paine, S. (ed.) (1981) *Six Children Draw*, London: Academic Press.

Paivio, A. (1971) *Imagery and Verbal Processes*, New York: Holt, Rinehart & Winston.

Papadakis, E. A. (1989) "Development of children's drawings in relation to gender and culture", unpublished PhD thesis, University of Birmingham.

Park, C. (1978) book review of *'Nadia: A case of extraordinary drawing ability in an autistic child'*, *Journal of Autism and Childhood Schizophrenia*, 8, (4), 457–72.

Phemister, M. R., Richardson, A. M. and Thomas, G. V. (1978) "Observations of young normal and handicapped children", *Child: Care Health and Development*, 4, 247–59.

Phillips, W. A., Inall, M. and Lauder, E. (1985) "On the discovery, storage and use of graphic descriptions", in Freeman, N. H. and Cox, M. V. (eds) *Visual Order*, Cambridge: Cambridge University Press.

Piaget, J. and Inhelder, B. (1956) *The Child's Conception of Space* (translated by F. J. Langdon and J. L. Lunzer), London: Routledge & Kegan Paul.

Piaget, J. and Inhelder, B. (1969) *The Psychology of the Child*, London: Routledge & Kegan Paul.

Pirenne, M. H. (1970) *Optics, Painting and Photography*, Cambridge: Cambridge University Press.

Premack, D. (1959) "Toward empirical behaviour laws: I. Positive reinforcement", *Psychological Review*, 66, 219–33.

Roback, H. B. (1968) "Human figure drawings: Their utility in the clinical pyschologist's armamentarium for personality assessment", *Psychological Bulletin*, 70, 1–19.

Rouma, G. (1913) *Le Langage Graphique de l'enfant*, Paris: Misch. et Thron.

Rubin, E. (1915) *Figure and Ground*, partial translation by Wertheimer, M. (1958), in Beardsley, D. C. and Wertheimer, M. (eds) *Readings in Perception*, New York: Van Nostrand.

Ryan, T. and Schwartz, C. (1956) "Speed of perception as a function of mode of representation", *American Journal of Psychology*, 69, 60–9.

Sacks, O. (1985) *The Man who Mistook his Wife for a Hat*, Great Britain: Gerald Duckworth & Co. Ltd.

Schaefer-Simmern, H. (1948) *The Unfolding of Artistic Ability*, Berkeley: University of California Press.

Schilder, P. (1935) *Image and Appearance of the Human Body*, London: Kegan Paul.

Schildkrout, M. S., Shenker, I. R. and Sonnenblick, M. (1972) *Human Figure Drawings in Adolescence*, New York: Brunner/Mazel.

Schiller, F. V. (1875) *Essays Aesthetical and Philosophical*, London: George Bell.

Schuyten, M. C. (1904) "De oorspronkelijke 'ventjes' der Antwerpsche schoolkinderen", *Paedologisch Jaarboek*, 5,1–87.

Scott, L. H. (1981) "Measuring intelligence with the Goodenough-Harris drawing test", *Psychological Bulletin*, 89, 483–505.

Sechrest, L. and Wallace, J. (1964) "Figure drawings and naturally occurring events: Elimination of the expansive euphoria hypothesis", *Journal of Educational Psychology*, 55, 42–4.

Selfe, L. (1977) *Nadia: A Case of Extraordinary Drawing Ability in an Autistic Child*, London: Academic Press.

Selfe, L. (1983) *Normal and Anomalous Representational Drawing Ability in Children*, London: Academic Press.

Silk, A. M. J. (1986) "Development and differentiation in children's figure drawings', unpublished PhD thesis, University of Birmingham.

Silk, A. M. J. and Thomas, G. V. (1986) "Development and differentiation in children's figure drawings", *British Journal of Psychology*, 77, 399–410.

Silk, A. M. J. and Thomas, G. V. (1988) "The development of size scaling in children's figure drawings", *British Journal of Developmental Psychology*, 6, 285–99.

Smilansky, S. (1968) *The Effects of Sociodramatic Play on Dis-*

advantaged Preschool Children, New York: John Wiley.

Smith, M. L. and Glass, G. V. (1977) "Meta-analysis of psychotherapy outcome studies", *American Psychologist*, 32, 752–60.

Solley, C. M. and Haigh, G. (1957) "A note to Santa Claus", Topeka Research Papers, *The Menninger Foundation*, 18, 4–5.

Strauss, M. (1978) *Understanding Children's Drawings*, London: Rudolf Steiner Press.

Swensen, C. H. (1957) "Empirical evaluations of human figure drawings", *Psychological Bulletin*, 54, 431–66.

Swensen, C. H. (1968) "Empirical evaluations of human figure drawings: 1957–1966", *Psychological Bulletin*, 70, 20–44.

Thomas, G. V., Chaigne, E. and Fox, T. (in press) "Children's drawings of topics differing in significance: Effects on size of drawing", *British Journal of Developmental Psychology*.

Thomas, G. V. and Tsalimi, A. (1988) "Effects of order of drawing head and trunk on their relative sizes in children's human figure drawings", *British Journal of Developmental Psychology*, 6, 191–203.

Treffert, D. A. (1989) *Extraordinary People*, London: Bantam Press.

Truax, C. B. and Carkhuff, R. R. (1967) *Toward Effective Counselling and Psychotherapy: Training and Practice*, Chicago: Aldine.

van Sommers, P. (1984) *Drawing and Cognition*, Cambridge: Cambridge University Press.

Vasari, G. (1912–14) *Lives of the Most Eminent Painters, Sculptors and Architects*, London: Medici Society.

Wallach, M. A. and Leggett, M. I. (1972) "Testing the hypothesis that a person will be consistent: Stylistic consistency versus situational specificity in size of children's drawings", *Journal of Personality*, 40, 309–30.

Wason, P. C. (1970) "On writing scientific papers", *Physics Bulletin*, 21, 407–8.

Willats, J. (1977) "How children learn to draw realistic pictures", *Quarterly Journal of Experimental Psychology*, 29, 367–82.

Willats, J. (1981) "What do the marks in the picture stand for? The child's acquisition of systems of transformation and denotation", *Review of Research in Visual Arts Education*, 13, 18–33.

Willats, J. (1984) "Getting the drawing to look right as well as to be right: The interaction between production and perception as a mechanism of development", in Crozier, W. R. and Chapman, A. J. (eds) *Cognitive Processes in the Perception of Art*, Amsterdam: Elsevier Science Publishers.

Willats, J. (1985) "Drawing systems revisited: The role of denotation systems in children's figure drawings", in Freeman, N. H. and Cox, M. V. (eds) *Visual Order*, Cambridge: Cambridge University Press.

Wilson, B. and Wilson, M. (1977) "An iconoclastic view of the imagery sources in the drawings of young people", *Art Education*, 30, 5-11.

Wiltshire, S. (1987) *Drawings*, London: J. M. Dent.

Wing, L. (ed.) (1976) *Early Childhood Autism*, (2nd edn) Oxford: Pergamon Press.

Winner, E. (1982) *Invented Worlds: The Psychology of the Arts*, Boston, Mass.: Harvard University Press.

Subject index

Name index